MW00794970

SECRET
LOS ANGELES

A Guide to the Weird, Wonderful, and Obscure

Danny Jensen

Reedy Press
PO Box 5131
St. Louis, MO 63139
www.reedypress.com

Library of Congress Control Number: 2019952737
ISBN: 9781681062167

Design by Jill Halpin

Printed in the United States of America
21 22 23 24   5 4 3 2

To Adrienne Florez, my love and fellow adventurer for life. Thank you for all of your support, encouragement, and assistance in running all over town to help make this book possible.

A big thanks to my amazing family for always cheering me on, not only for this venture, but throughout my life. I undoubtedly have you all to thank for my spirit of adventure, inquisitive nature, and sense of humor.

Thanks to my wonderful friends, both here in Los Angeles and around the world, for your support over the years and for joining me on so many capers near and far. Special thanks to Drew Lipman, Juliet Bennett Rylah, and Kris Miller for exploring many of the locations in this book with me, even when it meant hopscotching across the city in an afternoon.

Thanks to the amazing team at Reedy Press for helping to make this book a reality.

And a heartfelt thanks to all of the people, places, and organizations that make Los Angeles such a vibrant, exciting place to live and explore.

CONTENTS

INTRODUCTION

What happened to the original Venice canals? Where can you find the oldest tattoo parlor in the country? Where is the "Statue of Liberty of Los Angeles" perched? Is there a hidden wall surrounding LA? With *Secret Los Angeles* in hand, you'll discover the surprising answers to these curious mysteries and more.

Los Angeles is a city full of hidden histories, strange sculptures, and wonderful oddities that are often overlooked by locals and visitors alike. This book will serve as your guide to many of the most magical places across the city and surrounding county—places that you may never have noticed before or perhaps always wondered about.

For over a decade, I've researched and written about Los Angeles, I've led locals and visitors on countless food tours, and in my spare time, scoured and searched for fun and surprising places to explore. Though I may not have grown up here, from the first day I arrived, I was excited by all that Los Angeles has to offer. Now I'm thrilled to share my discoveries with you, and I hope that by learning the stories behind these hidden gems, you'll also gain a deeper and richer appreciation of the City of Angels.

To be clear, there's no way one book could capture all of the secrets of Los Angeles. While LA is often thought of as a city of Hollywood glamour and sprawling freeways, if you're willing to take the time to explore, you'll see that it's a place that runs deep with culture, history, and, yes, plenty of secrets. Each location that I researched and explored for this book, led me to uncover even more fascinating LA history. But I could only include so many places here, so think of this as a starting point in your journey. (You'll also find more places to explore in my first book, *100 Things to Do in Los Angeles Before You Die*, 2nd Edition, which I co-wrote with Carrie Kim about some of the most essential LA experiences.)

Learn a secret handshake over breakfast, sip top-shelf whisky while reciting poetry, or take a dip in the only natural hot spring in LA. Whether you've recently arrived or you're a longtime Angeleno, *Secret Los Angeles* will help you discover amazing places. You'll see the city in a whole new light—and have the chance to impress your friends and out-of-town guests.

THE *TRIFORIUM*

Did that spaceship-like sculpture behind City Hall once play music?

Standing proudly across the street from City Hall, the *Triforium* echoes the aspirational heights of its neighboring civic institution. Yet despite its colorful glass adornment and futuristic, interstellar ambitions, the public artwork has largely been scorned and neglected since it landed.

Built by mosaic artist Joseph Young and unveiled in 1975, the six-story-high, 60-ton sculpture consists of three concrete wishbone supports. The shape resembles a gallery that forms the upper story to the aisle of a church nave, known as a triforium. The structure is wrapped by three undulating waves of nearly 1,500 hand-blown Murano stained glass prisms arranged in vertical stripes of uniform color in a rainbow sequence. In addition to its wild aesthetic, the sculpture was designed to be an interactive musical instrument that synchronized light and sound—or in the artist's words, "the world's first polyphonoptic tower."

Young devised a computer system to illuminate incandescent bulbs behind each of the prisms in response to footsteps of pedestrians, conversations picked up by microphone, and music played on a keyboard connected to a 79-note Benjamin Franklin glass bell carillon in a nearby control room that piped notes through speakers on the *Triforium*. Young's wild vision also included laser beams that would project from the top

---

THE *TRIFORIUM*

What: A spaceship-shaped sculpture that synchronized light and sound

Where: Fletcher Bowron Square, 300 N. Main St. at E. Temple St.

Cost: Free

Pro Tip: Afterward, head to Grand Park, the tiered lawn on the other side of City Hall where you can relax on pink chairs and enjoy frequent events, including live music, yoga, food trucks, and more.

The three wishbone arches of Joseph Young's Triforium *took inspiration from LAX's Theme Building and symbolically represent the three branches of government. Photo by Danny Jensen.*

of the *Triforium's* pillars, pulsing out "Los Angeles" in Morse code to the galaxy as the "world's first ever astronomical beacon."

Young hoped the interactive instrument would reflect the kaleidoscopic nature of LA. Unfortunately, his design was ahead of its time and was plagued by difficulties from the start.

Over the years, burned-out bulbs had to be replaced regularly, and the sound system was glitchy from the get-go. Eventually, the *Triforium* was silenced in the 1980s due to noise complaints.

Thankfully, the *Triforium* has fans and supporters, and over the years, there have been several restoration efforts. Most notably, the Triforium Project brought the sculpture back online for a series of concerts in 2018. With further funding and support, the group aims to update the *Triforium* with brighter, longer-lasting, and more nuanced LED lights; a modern computer and sound system; and more interactive features that weren't possible in 1975.

Joseph Young, who passed away in 2007, also created several other public works throughout the city, including the six-pillar *Holocaust Monument* in Pan Pacific Park and the *Topographic Map*, a mosaic mural of LA County's water system on the side of the Hall of Records building downtown.

ANGELES CREST CREAMERY

Where can you hike with goats in the mountains?

Freely roaming farm animals may not be the first image that comes to mind for most people when they think of LA. But for those looking to connect with the region's agricultural past (and potential future), the Angeles Crest Creamery offers the chance to meet some charming, floppy-eared friends and get some exercise along the way.

Tucked away in the San Gabriel Mountains on the northern side of the Angeles National Forest, the 70-acre goat ranch is home to more than 60 Nubian goats—known collectively as a tribe. Run by Gloria Putnam along with her partner Christian Sariol, the ranch offers visitors the chance to take a leisurely hike with the tribe as they forage for food, nibbling sagebrush, scrub oak trees, rabbitbrush, and other plants. It's a unique and enchanting opportunity to hang out with goats, soak up the fresh air and beautiful chaparral landscape and surrounding pinyon-juniper woodland, and learn about Putnam and Sariol's efforts to develop a low-input, climate-change-resistant, and regenerative model for raising livestock.

Before starting Angeles Crest Creamery and discovering a passion for food production, Putnam trained as a physicist and worked in the semiconductor industry. While living on the historic Zane Grey Estate in Altadena, she bought two goats to have fresh milk on hand. Inspired by the experience, she began making cheese and teaching classes with the foodcrafting project, the Institute of Domestic Technology. When she wanted to expand, she bought the ranch in 2012, and she has been developing the project ever since.

Putnam recently purchased three acres across the road, including the old Mile High Cafe, which she plans to convert into a restaurant and cheese-making classroom. Just don't expect any goat yoga.

In addition to meeting the goats—which includes Grit, the male stud goat, and Rosie, Putnam's first goat—guests will also get to meet a pair of huge pet pigs (Katie and Abby), a pair of horses, Hank the donkey, turkeys, forty heritage chickens raised by Sariol, and four white Great Pyrenees dogs, who help protect the herd from coyotes. Photo by Danny Jensen.

ANGELES CREST CREAMERY

What: A goat farm hidden in the San Gabriel Mountains

Where: 19830 Big Pines Hwy.

Cost: Goat hikes start at $25.

Pro Tip: Pack a picnic to enjoy by the lake, and plan to purchase jars of ranch-made cajeta, a thick caramel syrup made from goat milk. Depending on availability, you can also buy fresh eggs, goat meat, goat cheese, ranch-roasted coffee, and natural body-care products.

Now you can join the goats on a short hike, typically offered two times each month (check the website for dates and be sure to book in advance) in addition to other special events, such as goat-milking classes, coffee-roasting, and more. If you're looking to spend even more time with the goats, you can stay at the ranch in a cozy cabin, one of two Airstreams, or in your own tent or RV. Overnight guests are invited to take part in a goat-milking lesson—not a typical LA weekend activity—and you'll also receive a taco kit with tortillas, beans, rice, pico de gallo, and, yes, slow-braised goat. They also offer potato tacos for vegetarians.

CHICKEN BOY

Where is the "Statue of Liberty of Los Angeles" perched?

Towering high above Figueroa Street in Highland Park stands *Chicken Boy*—a neighborhood icon and some say a fitting symbol for all things strange and wonderful about Los Angeles. Perched atop a squat, subtly Streamline Moderne commercial building, this feathered, fiberglass icon stands 22 feet tall with the head of a chicken and the brawny body of a man in blue jeans and a red shirt holding, of all things, a large bucket of chicken. With a proud, yet slightly startled look on his face—perhaps owing to the fact that he's hawking a bucket of his fellow fowl—*Chicken Boy* has come to be known as the "Statue of Liberty of Los Angeles." But it was a long, hard-fought journey to gain such revered status.

Chicken Boy's tale began in 1969, when he first roosted on the roof of an eponymous fried chicken restaurant on Broadway at 5th Street in Downtown LA. The imposing fellow was hatched by the International Fiberglass Company, a company founded in Venice that was responsible for countless giant, roadside statues often resembling Paul Bunyan, cowboys, and other characters, and referred to as Muffler Men.

Fittingly, it was just two blocks from what was once the western terminus of Route 66—that iconic roadway strewn with similarly kitschy relics of Americana—that he was first spotted in the mid-1970s by graphic designer Amy Inouye, at the time a recent newcomer to LA.

As fate would have it, Chicken Boy *returned to Route 66, where he began his journey decades ago in Downtown LA. Figueroa Street, where he now lives, had been part of the Transitional (1932–1934) and Alternate (1936–1940) Alignments of Route 66. It was later replaced in 1940 with the Arroyo Seco Parkway. Photo by Danny Jensen.*

Inouye considered *Chicken Boy* a welcoming presence, a new friend that represented the fun, playful, and innocent side of Los Angeles that was increasingly under threat by seriousness and sprawl. Then in May of 1984, Inouye discovered that the *Chicken Boy* restaurant had shuttered and the fate of its mascot, her friend, was in peril. After persistent inquiries, the building's realtor told her to come rescue the big bird if she wants it, and so Inouye hired a sign mover for a stealth operation to remove *Chicken Boy*. She thought she would be able to find a new home for her feathered friend at a museum or sculpture garden, but despite her best efforts, she couldn't find an interested party. So, for 23 years, *Chicken Boy* roosted in storage, but all the while his reputation grew thanks to press coverage, a short film, songs about him (including a polka!), and *Chicken Boy* souvenirs created by Inouye.

Then, thanks to a Community Beautification Grant and many jumps through bureaucratic hoops, *Chicken Boy* finally found his new home atop Inouye's business, Future Studio Design and Gallery in Highland Park. There his reputation as the Statue of Liberty of Los Angeles continues to grow, inspiring plenty of smiles and quizzical looks from passersby as he watches over us all.

In 2010, then-governor Arnold Schwarzenegger presented Amy Inouye and *Chicken Boy* the Governor's Historic Preservation Award. Look for *Chicken Boy*'s likeness on a small neon sign hung from the facade of the building, as well as a tile mosaic embedded in the sidewalk a block north.

THE MYSTIC MUSEUM

Where can you take classes on witchcraft and admire devilishly delightful art?

On a stretch of Magnolia Boulevard with a mostly wholesome "Main Street USA" vibe, you'll find a marvelously macabre museum dedicated to all things dark, weird, and spooky.

Even if you're not typically a fan of the occult, let your curiosity get the best of you at the Mystic Museum, its sister store, Bearded Lady Vintage & Oddities, and the new '80s-slasher-themed Camp Horror immersive retail space, and you're bound to be entranced by what you find. Owners Erick Yaro Wessel and Kiko Bailey have masterfully curated a collection of marvels to admire, including a permanent collection of oddities and rotating exhibits featuring works from local, national, and international artists. In the gift shop, you'll encounter everything from skulls and ethically sourced taxidermy to antique funerary art and spooky dolls. There are also new items, including artwork, séance candles, books on the occult, and plenty of playful gifts such as a teacup that says "I could poison you."

In the back of the shop, you'll find a door that leads to the museum's exhibit space, where you'll encounter incredibly elaborate set pieces, original artwork, movie props, and plenty of ghastly photo ops. Exhibitions typically run for three to four months before rotating out.

THE MYSTIC MUSEUM

What: A museum, gift shop, and event space dedicated to all things dark and spooky with plenty of camp thrown in for fun

Where: 3204 W. Magnolia Blvd., Burbank

Cost: Free to browse (though you'll probably end up buying something); exhibits are typically $150, and class prices vary.

Pro Tip: Check the Facebook page to learn about upcoming exhibits and classes.

Exhibits at the Mystic Museum have included an immersive horror experience celebrating the 40th anniversary of Evil Dead, *featuring actual props from the film, and "Slashback Video," an immersive homage to the horror section of long-gone mom-and-pop video shops of the '80s, complete with aisles of vintage VHS tapes of spooky classics and slasher films, as well as contemporary artists' interpretations of VHS covers. Photo courtesy of Mystic Museum.*

The Mystic Museum also hosts witchcraft classes, movie nights, séances, ghost investigations, psychic and tarot readings, and more. Plans are in the works for a fourth space, located down the block, which will likely feature Victorian-era exhibits, including an impressive collection of spirit boards, a variety of fortune-telling devices, antique devil collectibles, and "objects from the realm of the paranormal.

Before entering the Mystic Museum, spin the wheel of fortune (or misfortune) out front with forecasts such as "A witch watches over you," "You will be visited by a ghost," and "Wear all black all the time."

THE SKINNY HOUSE

Where can you find one of America's skinniest houses?

While LA might be known for sprawling celebrity mansions, one Long Beach house is defiantly famous for being the skinniest house in America—or at least in Southern California. Measuring just 10 feet wide across, the three-story, stuccoed home in the historic Rose Park neighborhood was built in 1932 simply to prove that the 10-by-50-foot lot on which it sits could be useful.

While tiny homes became a proper trend in the wake of our most recent housing crisis, it was the early years of the Great Depression that inspired a clever use of space at a time of limited resources. The narrow lot, created due to a surveying mistake, was first given to Newton P. Rummonds, an employee of a construction firm, in order to settle a $100 debt. While neighbors doubted that the patch of land could be put to good use, Rummonds aimed to prove them wrong. He hired local, unemployed construction workers to build a slender house on the lot as a means to advertise their talents.

The result was an 860-square-foot, English Tudor Revival-style abode with plenty of charming features, including a small enclosed front patio, double French doors, and a steep gabled roof with a single dormer. There's also a walled back patio and a roof deck. The home is currently occupied, so you can't get a close look at the interior's

THE SKINNY HOUSE

What: A record-holding Long Beach home that measures only 10 feet across

Where: 708 Gladys Ave., Long Beach

Cost: Free to see from the outside (it's currently occupied)

Pro Tip: Grab some hearty Mexican fare around the corner at Rivera's or a coffee and pastry at Rose Park Roasters at 3044 4th St.

The Skinny House will even look back at you—thanks to yellow, cat-like eyes currently peering out of the narrow upstairs windows. Photo by Danny Jensen.

stained-glass windows, the rooftop deck, or the beamed and vaulted ceiling in the bedroom. But nonetheless it's worth a visit to admire this skinny wonder from the outside.

While the Gladys Avenue home was once dubbed "America's Thinnest House" by "Ripley's Believe It or Not," the seven-foot-wide Hollensbury Spite House in Alexandria, Virginia, certainly gives it a run for its money. Meanwhile, in northern California, the Alameda Spite House matches its Long Beach counterpart at 10 feet wide. In fact, spite houses dot the countryside and globe, so named because they're intended to spite and annoy neighbors or city officials.

While the skinniest house in Long Beach is considered to be best suited for couples or single dwellers, reportedly a family of six somehow managed to squeeze in there in the 1950s.

THE BEACH BOYS
MONUMENT

Where can you pay tribute to the boys of summer?

No band has done more to spread the image of Southern California as a land of sun, fun, and waves than the Beach Boys. So it may come as a surprise to some fans to discover that the origin story of those breezy, laid-back vibes can be found tucked away alongside a freeway in a landlocked LA neighborhood. It's there on a quiet suburban street in Hawthorne, inside a humble tract house where the young brothers Brian, Dennis, and Carl Wilson, along with cousin Mike Love and friend Al Jardine, gathered to record their breakout hit, "Surfin'," over Labor Day weekend in 1961.

While the home was unfortunately demolished to make way for the 105 freeway in the 1980s, thankfully the site was designated as a California Historical Landmark. In 2005, a monument to commemorate the birthplace of the Beach Boys' legendary harmonies and surf-inspired

THE BEACH BOYS MONUMENT

What: The site of the childhood home of the band that brought the sun and fun of Southern California to the world

Where: 3701 W. 119th St., Hawthorne

Cost: Free

Pro Tip: Afterward, order up some soft serve at the nearby Foster's Freeze on Hawthorne Blvd., which some say is the hamburger stand mentioned in the Beach Boys song "Fun, Fun, Fun."

Brian Wilson received an F in his high school music class for writing what would later become "Surfin'." In 2018, when he was 75, his grade was changed to an A.

Whether you're a fan of the Beach Boys, music history, or just good vibrations in general, the monument is definitely worth a detour. Photo by Danny Jensen.

style was unveiled with Brian Wilson and Al Jardine in attendance along with David Marks, who joined the group later. While the street may be tricky to find, the monument is easy to spot when you arrive: a distinguished brick wall with a curved front, featuring a bronze plaque detailing the significance of the site and a large white stone bas-relief carving of the boys carrying a surfboard—an image that echoes the cover of their *Surfer Girl* album. The surrounding bricks feature the names of fans and local organizations that donated to the project, along with the names of the band members on plaques resembling 45s.

VERMONICA

Where can you see seven decades of streetlight designs in one place?

A row of streetlights in East Hollywood offers a glimpse back in time at historic LA streetlight designs while also raising questions about the nature of site-specific art.

Known as *Vermonica*, the art installation by artist Sheila Klein features 25 examples of the more than 400 different styles of lamps that have illuminated the city over the decades. There are designs from as far back as 1925, when the city's Bureau of Street Lighting was established, up until 1992.

Though we're often more aware of the glow provided by streetlights than the lamps themselves, in the early 1990s, Klein wanted to use streetlights to call attention not only to the lamps' design but also to what they lit up. "I decided to do something with streetlights because they have such a wonderful sculptural presence in the city and they are overlooked," she told the *Los Angeles Times* at the time.

While Klein initially envisioned an installation that could be seen from afar, such as Mulholland Drive, the project ultimately came to light on a grassy median in a strip mall parking lot in front of the since-closed Hollytron audio-video equipment store in East Hollywood. Klein chose the location because the streetside buildings of the strip mall had burned during the LA riots the year before. She was inspired by the idea of rebuilding after destruction, and with a $6,000 grant from the Cultural Affairs Department, additional funding from Hollytron, loaned streetlights from the Board of Public Works, and volunteer labor from the Bureau of Street Lighting, she created an "urban candelabra" in 1993. Located near the intersection of Vermont Avenue and Santa Monica Boulevard, the installation was given the portmanteau of Vermonica.

Originally planned to last only a year, *Vermonica* stood for 24 years due to its popularity. That suddenly changed in November of 2017, when the streetlights were uprooted and reinstalled two blocks away

The collection of streetlights features beautiful designs that have graced streets across the city, ranging from ornate Art Deco flourishes to slender, curved lamps. Photo by Danny Jensen.

VERMONICA

What: A deconstructed sculpture of historic streetlights

Where: 4584 Santa Monica Blvd.

Cost: Free

Pro Tip: To see more of LA's streetlight history, visit the Historic Street Lighting Museum at the Department of Public Works building in Downtown LA. The museum is open to the public by appointment one Friday each month (usually the second or third week) from 10 a.m. to 10:30 p.m.

in front of the Bureau of Street Lighting offices. Unfortunately, Klein was not notified, and she and others were understandably upset about the move. Klein felt that moving the streetlights from their original site-specific location removed an important context. In a statement she said "This is not my piece and it is no longer *Vermonica*."

Thankfully, however, after public outcry and support from preservationists and architect Loren Amador, *Vermonica* was restored to Klein's vision in 2020. Now located just a couple of blocks from the original site, the installation includes original details such as plaques naming each light. *Vermonica* is also now a part of the City Art Collection, so the installation's future is no longer in question and can be enjoyed for years to come.

Vermonica was created 15 years before artist Chris Burden installed the streetlights of *Urban Light* in front of the Los Angeles County Museum of Art.

AVENUE OF THE ATHLETES

Why are bronze plaques embedded in Echo Park's sidewalks?

The stars along Hollywood's Walk of Fame are known worldwide and visited by millions every year, but a little further east in Echo Park lies a series of bronze plaques embedded in the sidewalk along Sunset Boulevard that are barely noticed by most pedestrians. Known as the Avenue of the Athletes, these 32 plaques were the vision of the late L. Andrew Castle, once the team photographer for the Dodgers and longtime Echo Park booster. The small, often-overlooked rectangles line both sides of the boulevard for 10 blocks from Elysian Park Boulevard and Alvarado Street, and pay tribute to sports stars of the past, including numerous local legends.

Castle initially moved to LA to work in the silent film industry with the likes of Charlie Chaplin, but later turned his attention to photography and opened two camera shops—one in Echo Park and the other in Hollywood. Witnessing the throngs of tourists who came to see the Walk of Fame, Castle envisioned a similar attraction near his other store and, in 1974, he convinced the city to create one. Given that Dodger Stadium was just down the road, a walk dedicated to sports stars seemed appropriate.

The bronze plaques celebrate stars from 10 sports, including baseball, boxing, track, tennis, basketball, football, horse racing, swimming, diving, and golf, and they feature a symbol for the sport that corresponds to the athlete. LA sports fans will recognize familiar local legends, such as Dodgers pitcher Sandy Koufax and manager Tommy Lasorda, Kareem Abdul-Jabbar and Elgin Baylor of Lakers

---

Several other walks of fame dot the sidewalks of LA, including the Latino Walk of Fame in East LA, the RockWalk on the Sunset Strip, and the TV and Movie Animal Walk of Fame in Burbank.

Inside Dodger Stadium, the team has established an annual award in Andrew Castle's name for the best photo of the season by a local professional photographer. The winning pictures are displayed outside the press box. Photo by Danny Jensen.

AVENUE OF THE ATHLETES

What: A 10-block series of small bronze plaques, each honoring a sports legend, embedded in the sidewalk

Where: Sunset Boulevard, Echo Park

Cost: Free

Pro Tip: Explore the plaques before heading to a Dodgers game, and stop by the Short Stop bar for a pint and a tamale.

fame, and Jackie Robinson (who lived in Pasadena). But there are also plenty of plaques for athletes with little connection to LA, including track star Jesse Owens and boxer Joe Louis, who are among many other Olympians, along with tennis star Billie Jean King and others. Funding for the plaques was provided in part by the Dodgers along with other local business owners.

The first set of plaques were installed in 1976, followed by another batch the following year in what was to be an annual ceremony. But after Castle passed away in 1978, followed soon by his wife, the project lost steam until a final four plaques were installed in 1985, including one for Castle with an engraved camera. And while this collection of plaques may not hold the same notoriety and glitz as those to the west, they're nonetheless worth tracking down as you walk along Sunset.

THE BUTTERFLIES OF ABANDONED SURFRIDGE

Why do rare butterflies inhabit a ghost town near LAX?

If you've ever flown out of Los Angeles International Airport heading west during daylight hours, you may have wondered about the network of abandoned streets and empty lots between the end of the runway and the ocean. Once home to early Hollywood celebrities and well-heeled Angelenos, Surfridge is now the refuge of the endangered El Segundo blue butterfly, among other rare species. Fenced off from the public, all that remains of the once-exclusive estates and stylish homes are cracked roads, brush-covered lots, lonely palm trees, and lampless light posts.

First established in 1921 by real estate developer Fritz Burns of the firm Dickinson & Gillespie, Surfridge was built on miles of rolling sand dunes as an isolated retreat for the wealthy. In its initial years, it was also off-limits to anyone "not entirely that of the Caucasian race," according to the development's deed restrictions. The Great Depression ultimately sunk the initial project, but the prime oceanfront property continued to lure the rich and famous, which over the years included Cecil B. DeMille, Mel Blanc (the voice of Bugs Bunny), and Carmen Miranda.

It was a nearby airfield on a parcel of farmland that ultimately sealed the fate of Surfridge. Known as Mines Field, the airstrip drew crowds for air shows, but in 1928, the property became Los Angeles

---

THE BUTTERFLIES OF ABANDONED SURFRIDGE

What: A formerly wealthy neighborhood is now home to rare wildlife.

Where: Vista Del Mar, north of Imperial Highway, Playa Del Rey

Cost: Free

Pro Tip: Pack a picnic and enjoy the ocean views at a small park, but be prepared for jets flying over occasionally.

Plans are underway to eventually remove some of the streets, foundations, and streetlights of Surfridge and stock the area with more native plants, including poppies, salt grass, and sagebrush. Photo by Danny Jensen.

International Airport. As the airport expanded and jets became bigger and louder in the 1950s and 1960s, residents of Surfridge began to complain of deafening noise and falling soot as planes took off directly overhead. When lawsuits were filed, the city of LA declared eminent domain and began buying up homes in the community. While residents resisted, many ultimately relocated their houses to other neighborhoods, and others were forced out and their homes torn down. By the 1980s, the entire neighborhood, where more than 800 homes had once stood, was fenced off.

Before anything else could be done with the land, LAX officials discovered that the El Segundo blue butterfly—designated as endangered in 1976—was thriving on the coast buckwheat that grew on 200 acres of vacant Surfridge. So in 1986, the El Segundo Blue Butterfly Preserve was established to protect this unusual habitat not only for the butterfly but also for hundreds of other insect, plant, and animal species, including the rare burrowing owl. Conservationists are working to remove invasive species and reintroduce native ones. Although you currently can't explore beyond the fence around Surfridge, you can peer through to appreciate the area's latest residents who are enjoying a refuge in the rolling hills.

The El Segundo blue butterfly population once stretched across much of the 3,200 acres of El Segundo Dunes, which ranged from Santa Monica to Palos Verdes. It's estimated that the historic population included roughly 750,000 butterflies per year.

LOST SPIRITS DISTILLERY

Where can you find a wildly creative speakeasy-style distillery?

Take one part mad scientist's laboratory, add one part Willy Wonka's chocolate factory, and throw in a dash of Indiana Jones–style adventure, and you'll get a taste of what to expect at this most unusual and award-winning distillery. Because no ordinary setting would do for such a fantastical sounding venture, Lost Spirits Distillery is secreted away behind a mysterious door on an industrial stretch of the Arts District.

Founded by self-taught distillers Bryan Davis and Joanne Haruta, Lost Spirits began further north in Monterey County, but eventually found its way down to LA. The roughly two-hour, reservation-only tour includes a surprising welcome from TESSA, the monotone voice of an AI computer that helps run the distillery. The sci-fi beginning dives straight into fantasy, as a human guide invites you to sip a potent pour of the distillery's 61-proof, navy-style rum.

This is a tour best experienced first-hand, so I'll try and avoid giving away too much of the magic. The distillery also suffered a fire in 2019, but they were fortunately able to rebuild and return with even more elaborate experiences as you sample top-notch spirits and encounter wildly imaginative designs. Imagine, for instance, floating along a tropical river, reminiscent of Disneyland's Jungle Cruise, as you're whisked away toward the heart of the distillery.

You'll also encounter a high-tech laboratory where you'll learn a bit of fascinating chemistry. It's here where a reactor—referred to as a "time machine for booze"—uses powerful lights to break

---

Lost Spirits is using their innovative distillation techniques to rec-reate centuries-old booze that was supposedly sipped by the likes of Paul Revere and Napoleon by extracting compounds from old wood and yeast in the air.

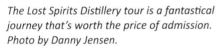

The Lost Spirits Distillery tour is a fantastical journey that's worth the price of admission. Photo by Danny Jensen.

down the chemical components of wood, which then combine with the molecules in the distilled alcohol to create the beloved flavors of 20-year-old, barrel-aged spirits in only six days. Not only does it sound impressive, the revolutionary technique creates rums and smoky, peated malt whiskies that are winning major awards.

And as if the wild tour and tasting weren't enough, at the end of the tour, you'll have the chance to buy some of those award-winning spirits to take home.

FACES OF ELYSIAN VALLEY

Why are there giant eggs with faces in a Cypress Park roundabout?

Perhaps the first question many Angelenos will have when encountering this unusual sight is, "What the heck is a roundabout?" A popular design in Europe and parts of the United States, but oddly rare in car-centric LA, the circular intersections are designed to improve traffic flow and safety as vehicles steadily move in one direction from multiple streets without traffic signals or stop signs. The design is so uncommon in LA that the city's first major, modern roundabout—the Riverside Roundabout—was only installed in 2017, in the neighborhood of Cypress Park. To make things more interesting, they turned the roundabout into a surreal work of public art known as *Faces of Elysian Valley.*

As you drive around the Riverside Roundabout, you're watched by nine stoic faces carved into massive granite-shaped eggs that look like they were placed there by an advanced alien race to ensure we could handle a roundabout. Located at the intersection of the Riverside Bridge, San Fernando Road, and Figueroa Street, the *Faces of Elysian Valley* sculptures were designed by Greenmeme Studio's Freya Bardell and Brian Howe.

FACES OF ELYSIAN VALLEY

What: Giant faces carved into nine huge granite eggs in the middle of a traffic roundabout

Where: N. Figueroa St. at San Fernando Rd. and Riverside Dr.

Cost: Free

Pro Tip: If you're driving, it's worth parking nearby and walking over to the roundabout to get a better look at the faces from across the street. There's no pedestrian access to the inside of the roundabout, so it's best to enjoy it from a safe distance.

The Faces of Elysian Valley were cut so that the eggs and the faces within them look like they're made of stacked geometric layers. The effect is reminiscent of those pin art toys where you can place your hand against the pins and the impression remained. The result is pretty trippy looking. Photo by Danny Jensen.

The massive pods, ranging in height from 8 to 12 feet, feature the likenesses of local residents who live in the surrounding Elysian Valley and who volunteered for the project. The designers used 3-D imaging to capture the images of the volunteers, which were then cut into locally sourced granite by Cold Spring Granite so that you see a face protruding from the inside of each egg and the inverse image on the back.

To avoid waste, multiple sculptures were carved from one block of stone with the front of the eggs lying in front of the faces, and the off-cuts used to create a giant sculptural ring around the eggs to protect them from traffic. In addition to improving traffic and safety and looking really cool, the Riverside Roundabout also helps divert stormwater runoff from the nearby LA River. There's a 25,000-gallon cistern buried beneath the roundabout, and the area was landscaped with water-wise local plants. It's not just a wild-looking sight, a tribute to the local community, and a smart traffic feature; it's eco-friendly as well.

If you look carefully at the granite ring surrounding the eggs, you'll see three more faces stretched along the perimeter.

THE MUSICAL ROAD

Where is there a road that plays an out-of-tune version of the "William Tell Overture" finale?

Though many of us log plenty of hours listening to music in our cars while stuck in traffic on LA's streets, it's rare that the road actually plays the music for you. Located in the far reaches of northern LA County, the city of Lancaster's Musical Road may be a bit of a road trip for some, but at least it comes with its own playlist.

As you drive west along Avenue G, just past 30 St. West, be sure to move over to the far left lane, roll down your windows, and listen for a completely out-of-tune rendition of the finale to Gioachino Rossini's "William Tell Overture"—or as some may know it, the theme song to *The Lone Ranger*.

Originally designed and created by Honda Motor Co. for a car commercial in September 2008, the roughly quarter-mile-long Musical Road was first located nearby on Avenue K. It was there that the car company collaborated with the city of Lancaster to cut grooves in the pavement, similar to rumble strips, so that when a car—a Honda Civic in the case of the commercial—drove over them at 55 mph, the tires would produce a series of pitches that played the dramatic conclusion of Rossini's symphony. A great marketing ploy to be sure, but unfortunately, the neighbors didn't agree. The Musical Road was paved over just 18 days after it was installed due to complaints from nearby residents of noise and dangerous traffic conditions from the newly popular road.

Thankfully, due to popular demand, the Musical Road was revived and relocated to a more remote location. The only problem—it's out

---

The Musical Road is considered the first of its kind in the United States, though there's now a stretch of Route 66 in New Mexico that plays "America the Beautiful," in addition to melodic roads in South Korea, Japan, and Denmark.

The Musical Road was originally designed by K. K. Barrett, production designer and former drummer for the LA techno-punk band the Screamers, who used 3/4-inch grooves to make it loud. Photo by Danny Jensen.

THE MUSICAL ROAD

What: A stretch of road that plays the "William Tell Overture" finale as you drive over it

Where: Avenue G, Lancaster

Cost: Free

Pro Tip: While in Lancaster, be sure to also check out the Antelope Valley Indian Museum, along with the Antelope Valley Poppy Preserve when the flowers are in bloom, typically around March to April.

of tune. When you drive along you'll hear a pretty wonky version of the song, even if you drive the recommended 55 mph. Those who drove the original road claim it had the same issue, and it was overdubbed for the commercial (Honda contends that it was designed specifically for the Civic's measurements, but we're not so sure). One theory is that the road was designed correctly, but that the rumble strips were spaced without accounting for the width of the grooves themselves, so the entire tune was thrown out of whack. Whatever the case, even out of tune, you'll still get a laugh out of driving down the Musical Road.

SPEAKEASY STORAGE

Was that towering public storage building really a speakeasy?

Stashing away your extra junk in a storage unit may seem like a modern concept, but the massive American Storage Building at Beverly Boulevard and Virgil Avenue proves that people have been hiding not just their possessions, but plenty of secrets as well, for much longer.

Built in 1928 by notable LA architect Arthur E. Harvey, the 13-story building features an eye-catching mix of Art Deco, Gothic, and Spanish Revival flourishes. Advertised at the time as "the most beautiful storage building in the world," it's clearly not your typical storage facility—but it was the illicit parties that took place at Prohibition-era speakeasies on the top floor that really set it apart.

On September 17, 1928, Erle W. "Curley" Bordwell opened The Roof Garden, a "nite club de luxe" that featured dancing, entertainment, and "unexcelled cuisine," according to a flyer at the time.

The party at The Roof Garden didn't last long, however, and in late December 1928, a new nightclub, known as Thirteenth Heaven took its place. In keeping with the theme, guests were greeted by "St. Peter," who whisked them up to the thirteenth floor, where they encountered winged waiters as well as musicians and attendants dressed in a way that was "intended to produce a spiritual illusion."

The parties on the top floor of the American Storage Building continued for years. Though likely due to frequent raids during

Prohibition, the club changed names several times. In 1931, it was dubbed the Los Angeles Press Club—not to be confused with the organization devoted to serious journalism in the city—but that operation was short-lived as federal prohibition agents raided the place, seizing 21 twelve-gallon crocks of beer mash, 203 bottles of beer, and "a complete plant for making beer."

The decades following the end of Prohibition proved to be much less eventful for the once-boisterous American Storage Building. These days, it's mostly home to other people's junk. And while the orange decorations and signage added by the Public Storage company, the building's current owner, might not be to everyone's taste, the company did repair significant damage to the ornate facade and added new elevators. Just don't expect St. Peter to greet you when you go to stash your belongings.

The American Storage Building is thought by some to be an inspiration for Disney's Tower of Terror (which has since been converted to another ride in Anaheim but lives on elsewhere) and not just because there are similar design elements. It's rumored that the mob, which may have had ties to the building's speakeasies, may have tossed victims from the roof or down an elevator shaft—not unlike the one in the ride that starts on the 13th floor—and echoes of their screams can still be heard to this day.

CAMERA OBSCURA

Where can you quietly spy on people using 19th-century technology?

While Palisades Park offers sweeping views of the Pacific and the spectacle of Santa Monica Pier, the narrow park also offers a hidden attraction that promises a unique perspective on the popular destination—and a bit of peace and quiet. Secreted away on the second floor of the park's Senior Recreation Center, the camera obscura is a 120-year-old optic device—based on designs from ancient Greece—that provides a 360-degree view of the surrounding area.

The term *camara obscuratio* is Latin for "dark room," but the concept at play here can be traced back more than 2,000 years before modern photography. Greek philosopher Aristotle discovered that by passing sunlight from a partial eclipse through a pinhole, the image was reversed on the ground. The concept was developed further by Leonardo da Vinci and Giovanni Battista della Porta, who used mirrors and convex lenses to manipulate images in a dark room. By the turn of the 20th century, devices like the camera obscura became popular draws at beachfront tourist destinations.

In 1898, Santa Monica mayor Robert F. Jones built and donated a camera obscura to the North Beach Bath House along the Santa Monica boardwalk. The device was a huge hit with beachgoers, who paid 10 cents to spy on the surrounding shoreline from the circular wooden shack on stilts. After a brief relocation to Westlake Park (now MacArthur Park) in 1899, it quickly returned

Santa Monica's camera obscura has helped fight crime on multiple occasions, once by helping to identify the license plate of a hit-and-run driver and another time by spotting a purse-snatching in progress.

Santa Monica's camera obscura is a vestige of attractions that once captivated Angelenos (there are only about 10 remaining in the United States and fewer than 100 in the world), and while it may have been replaced by much flashier diversions, its understated simplicity is refreshing and offers a bit of voyeuristic fun. Photo by Danny Jensen.

CAMERA OBSCURA

What: A device from 1898 that allows visitors to catch a 360-degree view of Palisades Park

Where: 1450 Ocean Ave., Santa Monica

Cost: Free

Pro Tip: To see another unique perspective, head across town to view the Griffith Observatory's camera obscura.

and was later bought by the city in 1910 and moved from the beach up to Linda Vista Park (now Palisades Park). In 1955, the device was moved into its current home inside the Senior Recreation Center.

To visit, show your ID and sign in at the front desk before heading upstairs. There, you'll find a small darkroom with a large, white circular board onto which panoramic images from the surrounding area are projected. A mirror located inside a turret on the roof reflects the surrounding scene, and a convex lens flips the image onto the board. Using a ship's wheel, you can turn the turret right and left to view the surrounding beach and park as well as Ocean Avenue. The images are slightly grainy, giving them a charming vintage quality, and viewing the outside world in silence is like a bit of meditation amid the surrounding bustle.

THE BEJEWELED WARNER BROS. THEATRE

Where can you find a hidden movie palace in Downtown LA's Jewelry District?

If you've ever ventured down to LA's Jewelry District—perhaps in search of a deal on an engagement ring or a shiny splurge—there's likely one building that stood out from the district's dozens. At the corner of 7th and Hill Streets proudly stands a spectacular steel-framed, nine-story Beaux Arts building with ornate moldings. Perhaps you wondered why there was a theater marquee boasting of "gold" and "diamonds" rather than the names of films and movie stars. And if you looked really carefully, you may even have noticed that the frame around the giant diamond in the center of the marquee seems to bear a striking resemblance to the Warner Bros. logo. But what you might not have done is step inside the building to discover the remnants of a 100-year-old movie palace.

Designed by architect B. Marcus Priteca, this hidden gem opened in 1920 as the Pantages Theatre a full decade before the existing namesake in Hollywood, and it featured vaudeville performances as well as films. This Pantages, much larger than the first built on Broadway, featured a 2,200-seat theater, shops, and offices on the upper floors.

THE BEJEWELED WARNER BROS. THEATRE

What: A historic movie palace disguised as a jewelry store

Where: 410 W. 7th St.

Cost: Free, assuming you don't buy any jewelry

Pro Tip: You're free to admire the theater's interior during normal business hours, but security does not take kindly to photography, so be discreet.

B. Marcus Priteca designed more than 200 theaters across the United States and Canada, including all of theaters for the Pantages vaudeville circuit from 1911 onward, as well as several other theaters in LA. Photo by Danny Jensen.

In 1929, amid a scandal, Alexander Pantages sold the theater to Warner Bros. The company quickly remodeled the building, adding new seating and a glitzy new marquee and replacing "P" with "WB" over the doorways. Over the decades, the theater remained a popular destination, eventually becoming a Stanley Warner theater in the late '50s, and then Warrens Theatre, before closing in 1975. It was briefly used as a church before transforming into the Jewelry Exchange (now known as the Jewelry Theater Center), home to multiple wholesale and retail vendors.

Thankfully, you can still head inside and see what remains of this once-grand movie palace. Make your way through the former lobby, where beautifully detailed archways remain, and head toward the back of the theater—past the glass cases of jewels—where you'll be greeted by a spectacular auditorium featuring baroque ornamentation, spacious box seats, and a classical mural on the ceiling. You can still see the "WB" over the doorways, look up to the large balcony, and stand where countless films were shown to the crowds.

You can admire other architectural wonders by B. Marcus Priteca by visiting the Fine Arts Theatre in Beverly Hills, the Warner Grand Theatre in San Pedro, and, of course, the Pantages in Hollywood.

OLD TOWN MUSIC HALL

Where can you watch silent films accompanied by a Wurlitzer organ?

In a city known for movie-making, there are surprisingly few places to see the classic films of Hollywood up on the big screen. Fortunately, the silver screen gems of old are brought to life every weekend at the Old Town Music Hall in El Segundo. Not only does the intimate, charming theater show the beloved films of the Golden Era, but you can also enjoy silent films and cartoons accompanied by music and sound effects from a massive Mighty Wurlitzer theater pipe organ.

First opened as the State Theatre in 1921 following a building conversion by noted engineer Edward L. Mayberry Jr., the 200-seat theater (now 188 seats) was designed to be a live entertainment venue for the workers at the nearby Standard Oil refinery. It showed films until the mid-1930s, when it closed. It reopened in 1944 as the El Segundo Theatre and was later renamed the State Theatre in 1957.

Then, in the late 1960s, the theater underwent a magical transformation. Two local musicians, Bill Coffman and Bill Field, rented the space and installed a Mighty Wurlitzer, which the "Two Bills" rescued from the shuttered Fox West Coast Theatre in Long Beach and meticulously restored and rebuilt. Hugely popular during the silent era of film as it could imitate the music of a full orchestra, the large pipe organ is quite a delight to see—and hear!

When the velvet curtain opens, you'll see more than 2,600 pipes, colorfully illuminated thanks to black lighting, along with a xylophone, drums, cymbals, horns, bells, gongs, and more. The

The theater also has a beautiful nine-foot Bösendorfer concert piano, handmade in Vienna for the Old Town Music Hall, which is used for live concerts, including jazz and ragtime.

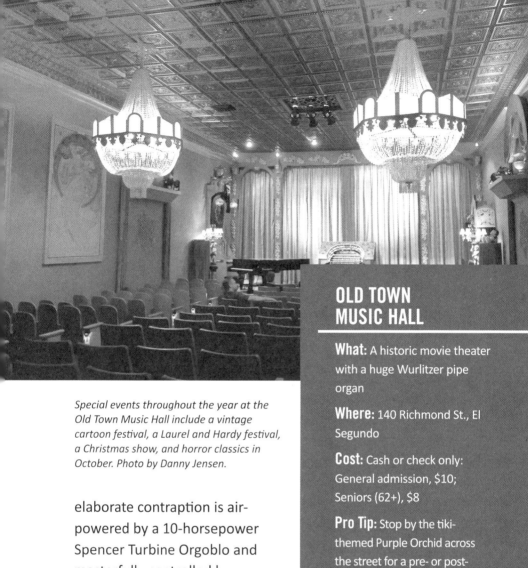

Special events throughout the year at the Old Town Music Hall include a vintage cartoon festival, a Laurel and Hardy festival, a Christmas show, and horror classics in October. Photo by Danny Jensen.

OLD TOWN MUSIC HALL

What: A historic movie theater with a huge Wurlitzer pipe organ

Where: 140 Richmond St., El Segundo

Cost: Cash or check only: General admission, $10; Seniors (62+), $8

Pro Tip: Stop by the tiki-themed Purple Orchid across the street for a pre- or post-show tropical cocktail.

elaborate contraption is air-powered by a 10-horsepower Spencer Turbine Orgoblo and masterfully controlled by an organ console with four keyboards, 260 switches, and numerous controls and pedals. While the talented Bill Coffman passed away in 2001 and Bill Field died in June of 2020, Field's young protégé Edward Torres carries on the tradition as the resident organ player.

Each show at the Old Town Music Hall, performed Friday through Sunday, features music played on the Wurlitzer, an audience sing-a-long, a comedy short (often a cartoon) with music and sound effects from the organ, and a feature film—often from the Golden Age of Hollywood, though occasionally a silent movie.

THE FUNKIEST CHICKEN SHACK

Why does that KFC on Western Avenue look like a postmodern bucket of chicken?

Or is it a giant postmodern chicken? It's neither, according to the architects who designed the unique fast-food joint at the southeastern corner of East Hollywood just above Koreatown, but it's certainly funky. Monstrosity or marvel depending on who you ask, the wild-looking building grabs the eye as you drive by on Western Avenue, just north of Beverly Boulevard, with its chunky, asymmetrical geometric shapes and vague resemblance to architect Frank Gehry's iconic Disney Concert Hall. So, how did this one-of-a-kind bird come to be?

In the late 1980s, KFC franchisee Jack Wilkee wanted to shake things up with a redesign of his 25-year-old restaurant. "I challenged the notion that all KFC franchises should have the same standard design of fake mansard roofs (and) outsize Colonel Sanders bucket," he explained to the *Los Angeles Times*. To achieve his vision, Wilkee, an art collector and admirer of modern architecture, turned to architects Jeffrey Daniels and the late Elyse Grinstein, who had met at Frank Gehry's office. While the pair took cues from Gehry (whose concert hall wouldn't appear until more than a decade later), they were also inspired by the dramatic designs of Googie-style architecture of the 1950s.

THE FUNKIEST CHICKEN SHACK

What: A wild-looking KFC, designed by two notable LA architects

Where: 340 N Western Ave.

Cost: Free, not counting the bucket of fried chicken you may be tempted to buy

Pro Tip: Before grabbing a bucket at the KFC, head diagonally across Western Avenue to wet your whistle at Blipsy Bar at 369 N. Western Ave., an unmarked bar packed with vintage arcade games and pinball machines.

While the architects intended to design a constructivist building, many have interpreted it as a modernist spin on programmatic architecture (along the lines of the hat-shaped Brown Derby restaurant) thanks to its resemblance to a bucket of chicken. Photo by Danny Jensen.

Perched on the street corner, the two-story structure, built between 1989 and 1990, features a giant curved stucco wall with large metal fins (which act as solar shades for windows) soaring vertically. The curve collides with a large block of corrugated metal on one side and serves as a shield for a second-floor-balcony seating area on the other. High atop the building sits a red cube-shaped cupola, seemingly precariously placed on the edge, featuring the familiar face of the Colonel beckoning you into this fast-food fun house.

While some say the building resembles a giant bucket of chicken, others insist it's meant to look like a chicken with the metal fins as wings and the red cube serving as the head. Meanwhile, the architects claimed that they didn't intend for it to resemble either. It's "just a chicken shack," the pair told the *Los Angeles Times*. Whatever you call it, you're not likely to find another fast-food joint like it.

Elyse Grinstein and Jeffrey Daniels, the fine-feathered architects behind the KFC, also designed artist David Hockney's Hollywood Hills home.

THE BLACK CAT TAVERN

Where did one of the first LGBTQ civil rights demonstrations in the country take place?

While it may look like just another bustling gastropub these days, the Black Cat in Silver Lake was the site of what's considered the first documented large-scale LGBTQ civil rights protest in the United States. While New York's monumental Stonewall uprising in 1969 is more widely known as a flashpoint in the fight for equal rights, the pivotal events that took place here in LA occurred two years earlier and helped set the stage for what was to come.

Located on Sunset Boulevard near Sunset Junction, the Black Cat Tavern in the 1960s was a gay bar with a largely working-class clientele. Just after midnight on New Year's Day 1967, as bar patrons shared celebratory kisses and embraces, eight undercover police officers who had infiltrated the bar began arresting patrons, beating and dragging many into the street. Fourteen people were charged with lewd conduct for same-sex kissing. At the time, sex between two men was illegal in California, and a conviction of lewd conduct required registering as a sex offender.

In response to the raid and unprovoked violence, activists organized what is considered one of the earliest known demonstrations for LGBTQ rights. On February 11, 1967, an estimated 500 to 600 people gathered with picket signs to peacefully protest the raid, as well as the ongoing harassment of the LGBTQ community, criminalization of same-sex relations, and police brutality from the LAPD. Two organizations—the Personal Rights in Defense and Education (PRIDE) and the Southern California Council on Religion and the Homophile (SCCRH) came together to help

In 2008, The Black Cat became the first building in Los Angeles to be landmarked solely for its role in LGBTQ history.

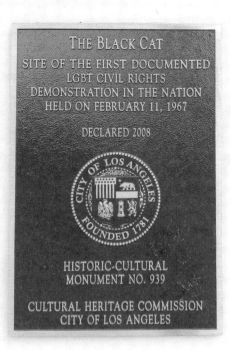

Two of the men arrested during the Black Cat raid were ultimately convicted of lewd conduct, and their court case had significant legal implications. It was the first time in US history that gay men were defended under the equal protection clause of the 14th Amendment. Photo by Danny Jensen.

THE BLACK CAT TAVERN

What: The site of the first documented large-scale LGBTQ civil rights protest in the United States

Where: 20 Westminster Ave., Venice

Cost: Free to see from the outside, currently occupied

Pro Tip: To learn more LGBTQ history, be sure to visit ONE National Gay and Lesbian Archives at USC.

organize the protest, along with many others.

Since the historic demonstration, the bar has closed and reopened under a variety of names over the years. In 2008, the site was designated a Los Angeles Historic-Cultural Monument for its role in the LGBTQ civil rights movement and received a small bronze plaque on the side of the building. The building reopened in 2012 as The Black Cat, a gastropub.

WALT DISNEY'S CAROLWOOD BARN

Where can you find the birthplace of Imagineering that gave rise to the Disney empire?

Even though Disneyland is located in Orange County, you can actually step inside the room—or more specifically, the barn—where it's believed that Walt Disney first dreamed up many of the ideas for the theme park that would capture the world's imagination. Located at the northern tip of Griffith Park, the Carolwood Barn offers kids of all ages the chance to peer inside the birthplace of many of Disney's visions, plus the opportunity to ride on a miniature railroad just as Walt did.

Originally constructed in 1950 behind Disney's home on Carolwood Drive in Holmby Hills, the Carolwood Barn was the station building for his miniature railroad. From within the barn, Walt could monitor and control the switches for his 1/8th-scale tracks that ran for 2,615 feet, which included a 46-foot-long trestle bridge and a 90-foot tunnel that ran beneath his wife Lillian's flower garden. Besides operating the railroad, Walt would spend hours in the barn, which doubled as a workshop, both alone and with friends and fellow animators, thinking up new projects and ideas. The barn is considered by many to be the birthplace of Imagineering, the creative engine (fittingly) that designs and builds all Disney theme parks, attractions, resorts,

WALT DISNEY'S CAROLWOOD BARN

What: The workshop where Walt dreamed up ideas for Disneyland and operated his scale-model live-steam railroad

Where: 5202 Zoo Dr.

Cost: Free, though donations are strongly encouraged

Pro Tip: Pack a picnic to enjoy on the benches and picnic tables near the barn.

To complete the railroad experience, be sure to check out the Live Steamers Railroad Museum and climb aboard a working model steam engine that loops around the barn and surrounding property. Nearby, there's also Travel Town, which features retired full-size steam engines, railroad cars, and models. Photo by Danny Jensen.

cruise ships, and more. Many of Disney's first animators and Imagineers were also railroad enthusiasts, and some had backyard railroads of their own.

When the Holmby Hills home was sold, after Walt and Lilly passed away, their daughter Diane Disney Miller helped rescue the barn from demolition. The barn was entrusted to Michael and Sharon Broggie, founders of the Carolwood Society, and eventually found a new home in Griffith Park in 1999, alongside the Los Angeles Live Steamers Railroad Museum.

The Carolwood Barn is now home to a small museum, operated by the Carolwood Society, dedicated to Walt's love of trains and model railroading, and features memorabilia from the creation and early days of Disneyland. Outside the barn, you'll also find one of the original Disneyland & Santa Fe Railroad cars, which pulled into Main Street Station when Disneyland opened on July 17, 1955.

The barn is open on the third Sunday of each month from 11 a.m. to 3 p.m. with free parking and admission. It's considered the only regularly operating Disney attraction in the world that is completely free—though donations are appreciated.

When Walt first moved to LA, he briefly rented a room in the home of his uncle and aunt in nearby Los Feliz at 4406 Kingswell Ave., where he animated short films in the garage.

EL ALISAL (THE LUMMIS HOME AND GARDENS)

Where can you find a miniature castle hidden among sycamore trees?

Just off the Arroyo Seco Parkway (aka the 110) in Highland Park hides a stone castle built by Charles Fletcher Lummis, an eccentric Renaissance man and founder of Los Angeles's first museum. Known as El Alisal, named for the ancient sycamore tree that once stood in its courtyard, the unique home also hosted some of LA's wildest parties of the early 20th century and is now a museum that offers a fascinating look at Lummis's life and work.

Not one to shy away from the dramatic, Lummis famously walked from Cincinnati to Los Angeles in 1884, after dropping out of Harvard at 25 to take up a job as the first city editor for the fledgling *Los Angeles Times*. Along the way, he sent dispatches of his adventure to the paper, which were widely reprinted and helped him gain national notoriety. An obsessive worker and heavy drinker, Lummis was partially paralyzed after suffering a stroke, and he moved to New Mexico to recuperate. He later returned to LA as the editor of the magazine *Land of Sunshine* (later called *Out West*) where he advocated for the Southwest's indigenous cultures, as well as the region's Spanish heritage.

Beginning around 1896, Lummis began the roughly 13-year project of constructing El Alisal on the west bank of the Arroyo Seco River using river rock and discarded railroad telegraph poles. The Arts and Crafts wooden features helped embellish the already fairy-tale-like designs of the two-story castle, which features towers and narrow

Among the home's many incredible details, be sure to check out the window panes that feature glass-plate images of Lummis's photographs.

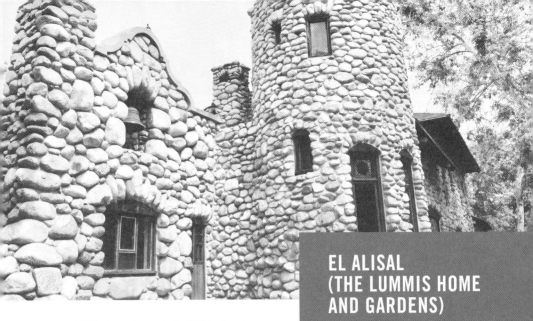

EL ALISAL (THE LUMMIS HOME AND GARDENS)

What: A stone castle built by eccentric Renaissance man Charles Lummis, featuring art and artifacts of the Southwest

Where: 200 E. Avenue 43

Cost: Free

Pro Tip: Check out the Lummis Days Festival, typically held in early June, which celebrates the art, music, history, and diversity of Northeast LA.

While legend says he built it by hand, Lummis did have help, including from Native American artisans and artists such as Maynard Dixon. Photo by Danny Jensen.

windows. El Alisal, and Lummis himself, became legendary for salon-like parties—which he called "noises"—featuring a lengthy roster of famous intellectuals, artists, and socialites. (Be sure to check out the impressive guest book when you visit.) In 1907, Lummis founded the Southwest Museum, considered LA's first museum, to showcase art and artifacts from the region.

Guided tours at El Alisal offer the chance to explore this unique architectural wonder, see many of the Southwestern artifacts Lummis collected, and learn about his storied life. Lummis was not without his faults, of which you'll also learn on the tour, but he undoubtedly left an impact on LA that is worth exploring. You'll also want to take time to explore the surrounding experimental gardens aimed at highlighting water conservation. The house is open Saturdays and Sundays from 10 a.m. to 3 p.m., and admission is free.

EL BORDELLO ALEXANDRA

Why are there gargoyles covering a house near Venice Beach?

The Venice Beach Boardwalk is home to plenty of colorful characters, but there's one apartment building that manages to really stand out from its neighbors. Located just off the boardwalk, the building known as El Bordello Alexandra is impossible to miss with its bold purple siding, gold and black iron work, and multitude of ghoulish gargoyles, medieval guards, and all manner of mythical figures, including Poseidon and a giant centaur, that cover all sides of the building. If a caped villain suddenly appeared on the second floor balcony, it would hardly seem out of place.

Built in 1906, the seven-unit apartment building is thought to have once been an actual bordello, according to ledgers found in the attic. For years, the storied structure was also rumored to be a heroin den run by a slumlord—that is, until Tony Wells and Brittany Stevenson bought and renovated the 5,000-square-foot building as an investment in 2001. In addition to completely gutting the building and giving it an extensive renovation, the couple took to decorating the property with a wildly eclectic mix of décor that they've sourced from their travels, both local and beyond. While the pair initially embraced the bordello theme, they say the design has taken on a life of its own with an ever-evolving look.

EL BORDELLO ALEXANDRA

What: An elaborately decorated apartment building covered with gargoyles and mythical beings

Where: 20 Westminster Ave., Venice

Cost: Free to see from the outside, currently occupied

Pro Tip: While the building is not open to the public, you may see some of the residents hanging out front. Don't be afraid to say hello—they're a friendly bunch.

The name Alexandra honors a late friend of the owners, whose likeness is immortalized on a mural on the facade. Photo by Danny Jensen.

Not surprisingly, El Bordello Alexandra is home to a tight-knit collection of artists and musicians who have a strong sense of community and often travel together to events such as Burning Man. Despite all the sinister-looking décor, El Bordello Alexandra feels like the most welcoming home on the block. And it's certainly a testament to Venice's long-standing artsy and funky vibe, which seems to be in shorter supply these days.

The Poseidon and centaur statues on the roof came from a metal shop in Mexico that creates sculptures from salvaged scraps.

THE SHAKESPEARE BRIDGE

How did the Bard wind up in Los Feliz?

Los Angeles is home to countless beautiful, historic, and awe-inspiring bridges, from San Pedro's soaring Vincent Thomas Bridge to the LA River–spanning Cesar Chavez Avenue Viaduct to Pasadena's curved Colorado Street Bridge. But one of the county's most charming bridges is not quite as well known or heavily trafficked as many of the rest.

Built in 1926 and originally known as the Franklin Avenue Bridge, the narrow span is just 260 feet long and 30 feet wide—just enough for one lane of traffic in each direction. Designed by city engineer J. C. Wright, the bridge was built to cross a ravine where the Arroyo de la Sacatela, a perennial stream, once flowed, connecting the hilly neighborhood of Franklin Hills with the rest of Los Feliz. While nobody seems to know just how the gothic-style passageway came to be known as the Shakespeare Bridge, there's a good chance the moniker was inspired by the bridge's whimsical, Elizabethan-like arched turrets with pointed roofs

At one point, the historic crossing was known as the Disney Bridge, due to the fact that Walt and his brother Roy lived close by and the Walt Disney Studios were just a little further down the road where Gelson's Market stands today.

While rumors that the Shakespeare Bridge appeared in The Wizard of Oz *have been widely debunked, the bridge was featured in* Dead Again, *directed by and starring Shakespeare superfan Kenneth Branagh. Photo by Danny Jensen.*

on each side (what some call aedicules), and the three open spandrel arches beneath.

In 1974, the city recognized the Shakespeare Bridge as a historic landmark, and it was retrofitted for earthquakes to the tune of $1.5 million in 1998. A stroll over the bridge gives you the chance to see the crossing's charming features up close, but be prepared for the narrow walkway that's only on one side.

THE DUNBAR HOTEL AND CENTRAL AVENUE'S JAZZ LEGACY

Where did Ella Fitzgerald, Duke Ellington, and other jazz legends stay when they played in LA?

Cities such as Chicago, New Orleans, and New York may spring to mind when you think of jazz history, but ask any serious fan of the genre, and they'll tell you that the thriving hub of West Coast jazz from the 1920s to the 1950s was LA's very own Central Avenue. And the beating heart of that musical scene was the Dunbar Hotel, a destination that played a significant role in LA's African American community for decades.

The Dunbar was first opened in 1928 as the Hotel Sommerville by husband and wife John and Vada Sommerville, two prominent dentists and civil rights activists. The couple planned the opening of the hotel to coincide with the NAACP's first West Coast convention that same year to provide first-class accommodations to African Americans who would otherwise be denied the same level of lodging elsewhere in segregated Los Angeles. Considered one of the finest black hotels in the nation, it helped ignite development in the area. Following the stock market

THE DUNBAR HOTEL AND CENTRAL AVENUE'S JAZZ LEGACY

What: A historic hotel that once hosted countless jazz legends where you can still hear music

Where: 4225 S. Central Ave.

Cost: Depends on how much you order at Delicious at the Dunbar

Pro Tip: Be sure to head across the street to the Central Avenue Jazz Park to check out the colorful tile mural created by kids and artists to celebrate the jazz legends of Central Avenue.

Each July, the Central Avenue Jazz Festival brings live jazz back to the streets of historic Central Avenue with music, dancing, art, and more. Photo by Danny Jensen.

crash of 1929, the Sommervilles lost the hotel, and it was bought by Lucius Lomax, who renamed it after poet Paul Laurence Dunbar.

In 1931, a nightclub with live music opened in the Dunbar Hotel, and in the decades to follow, the hotel played host to many of the country's most prominent black musicians.

A litany of jazz legends stayed and played at the Dunbar, including Duke Ellington, Louis Armstrong, Billie Holliday, Ella Fitzgerald, Nat King Cole, Count Basie, and Bessie Smith. The hotel also welcomed notable athletes, entertainers, and writers, including Joe Louis, Jack Johnson, Josephine Baker, Paul Robeson, and W. E. B. Dubois. The hotel was a focal point among more than a dozen jazz venues along Central Avenue, including hotspots such as Club Alabam, the Last Word, the Down Beat, and the Lincoln Theatre (considered the "West Coast Apollo"), and was surrounded by many other black-owned businesses that stretched from around 8th Street to Slauson Avenue.

While the Dunbar began to decline in the early 1960s, the hotel was recognized as an LA Historic Cultural Monument in 1974 and recently underwent a $30 million renovation. The building now provides affordable housing for seniors as well as a gathering place for the community.

While you can no longer stay at the hotel, you can head to Delicious at the Dunbar, a restaurant within the building, to enjoy Mexican and Southern fare and hear live jazz on weekends.

VALLEY RELICS MUSEUM

Where can you explore a living time capsule of the San Fernando Valley?

While much of LA's story is one of reinvention—building something new and tearing down the old—there's one institution dedicated to preserving the treasures of LA's San Fernando Valley that might have otherwise disappeared completely. The Valley Relics Museum features an enormous collection of historic artifacts, including neon signs, menus and ashtrays from long-gone restaurants, film and TV memorabilia, vintage arcade games, one-of-a-kind cars, and lots more.

The enchanting nonprofit museum is largely the work of one man, Tommy Gelinas, who grew up in the San Fernando Valley and for more than two decades has passionately and obsessively collected the endangered ephemera of the Valley and beyond. What began as a personal collection in his garage eventually grew into a museum—first in a Chatsworth warehouse in 2013, and then in a much larger space inside two airplane hangars at the Van Nuys Airport in 2018. Over the years, the museum has also received donations from Valley residents, enthusiasts, and celebrities. The current location houses roughly 25,000 items, which is only about a third of the entire collection.

The gift shop of the Valley Relics Museum is a treasure trove for anyone nostalgic for icons of the Valley and other Southern California favorites. Visitors can take home (or order online) mugs, T-shirts, and, in some cases, even small illuminated signs for restaurants and destinations that include Pioneer Chicken, The Palomino Club, Pup 'n' Taco, and the Saugus Speedway.

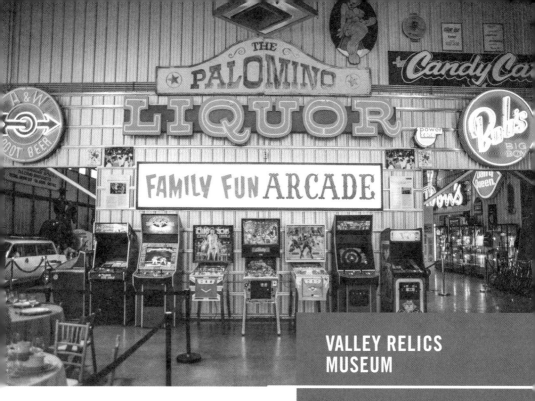

VALLEY RELICS MUSEUM

The Valley is often maligned as a suburbia devoid of culture and history, but the museum stands as a testament to the contrary. Photo courtesy of the Valley Relics Museum.

What: A massive and colorful collection of historic and pop culture artifacts from the San Fernando Valley

Where: 7900 Balboa Blvd., Lake Balboa, Hangar C 3 & 4

Cost: Adults, $10; Seniors, $8; Children 10 and under, free

Pro Tip: Be sure to check the museum's website and Facebook page for special events, which can include guest lecturers and bus tours to legendary Valley locations.

Even if you didn't grow up in the Valley, or in LA at all, there's plenty of Americana to enjoy. Likely to catch your attention first is the wall of neon and illuminated signs from some of the region's iconic destinations such as Van der Kamp's Bakery, The Palomino Club, and Henry's Tacos. You'll also want to check out the costumes and memorabilia from the many Westerns filmed in the Valley, a gold lamé "Nudie" suit worn by Elvis, the huge collection of BMX bicycles (many of which were made in the area), and yearbooks, historic letters, and countless photographs.

THE VELASLAVASAY PANORAMA

Where can you enjoy some good, old-fashioned Victorian entertainment?

Hugely popular during the late 18th and 19th centuries, mostly in Europe and the United States, panoramas (also known as cycloramas) surrounded viewers with a large, 360-degree cylindrical painting. In some cases, the painting also featured faux terrain in the foreground, while natural light was used to give the illusion of movement. The intricately detailed paintings often depicted battle scenes, religious stories, or idyllic landscapes, and could sometimes be as tall as 40 feet high and stretch 360 feet around. While the rise of cinema largely spelled the end of the public's fascination with panoramas, there's one place in LA where you can still experience the mesmerizing, immersive art form.

Located inside a historic movie theater (ironically enough), the Velaslavasay Panorama features an exhibition hall with what's considered the only 360-degree panorama west of the Mississippi, along with a theater, exhibit space, and a wild, enchanting garden in back. To view the panorama, you'll go up a small wooden staircase to find yourself completely surrounded by the Shengjing Panorama, a highly detailed painting of Shenyang city in Northeast China from the years 1910 to 1930, a transitional time for architecture, culture, and religion.

THE VELASLAVASAY PANORAMA

What: An immersive panorama painting inside a historic theater

Where: 1122 W. 24th St.

Cost: $7 suggested donation; students and seniors, $5

Pro Tip: Sign up for their mailing list to find out about cool special events that take place in the theater and garden.

The Union Theatre, the Velaslavasay Panorama's home, was built in 1910 and is one of the earliest purpose-built cinema houses in LA. Photo by Danny Jensen.

As you make your way around the viewing platform, examining the painting and the three-dimensional terrain and figures in the front, you'll hear the sounds of a bustling city from live field recordings, as the lighting subtly shifts from day to night. It's a magical and meditative experience that's difficult to describe. At a time when virtual reality is on the rise, the Velaslavasay Panorama feels timely and yet refreshingly analog.

The Shengjing Panorama launched in 2019 and is expected to run for years. Prior to that, the space featured a fantastical Arctic landscape known as "Effulgence of the North," which was created by artist and Velaslavasay Panorama founder Sara Velas. Be sure to check out the ancillary salon space, which features Nova Tuskhut, an Arctic trading post you can enter, as well as the garden.

BIDDY MASON
MEMORIAL PARK

Where can you find a peaceful park in the middle of Downtown LA that pays tribute to an inspiring Angeleno?

Tucked away from the bustle of Broadway near Grand Central Market hides a small memorial park that pays tribute to a remarkable woman and an influential figure in 19th-century Los Angeles, Bridget "Biddy" Mason.

Born into slavery in 1818, most likely in Georgia (though little is known of her early years), Mason spent much of her young adult life enslaved by Robert Smith, a Mississippi Mormon convert. In 1848, Smith decided to move his family and slaves to help establish the Mormon community in Salt Lake City. Mason, 30 at the time, traveled the roughly 1,700 miles on foot behind a 300-wagon caravan, while also cooking meals, herding cattle, serving as a midwife, and caring for her three young daughters.

Then in 1851, Smith again moved the household to San Bernardino, California—a state that had recently entered the Union and where slavery was illegal. Before Smith could relocate to slavery-permitting Texas, he was stopped by Charles Owens, who was romantically involved with Mason's oldest daughter. With the help of Owens's family and others, Mason fought for her freedom in court as Smith was keeping her as a slave illegally. On January 21, 1856, Mason and 13 members of her extended family were declared free.

Mason moved to Los Angeles with her family, where she worked as a midwife and nurse, earning a reputation for her

In 1872, Mason helped found the First African Methodist Episcopal Church of Los Angeles, the oldest church in LA founded by African Americans.

Mason won her freedom a year before the Dred Scott Decision when the US Supreme Court ruled that that no black person, free or slave, could claim US citizenship, and therefore were unable to petition the court for their freedom.

BIDDY MASON MEMORIAL PARK

What: A small park dedicated to one of the first African American women in LA to own land

Where: 333 S. Spring St.

Cost: Free

Pro Tip: You can also get to the Biddy Mason Memorial Park by exiting through the backdoor of the Bradbury Building, and you can admire the stunning architecture of the 1893 landmark along the way.

exceptional skills. She tended the sick in the county hospital and jail, and most famously as a midwife delivered hundreds of babies, including those of LA's wealthy and poor families.

After 10 years, Mason had saved an estimated $250 to purchase land for a homestead, becoming one of the first African American women to own property in Los Angeles. Her home was between Spring Street and Fort Street (later Broadway), and between 3rd and 4th Streets. In the years to come, Mason bought more property and became known as a benefactor of the poor and a community leader.

Located on the site of her homestead, the Biddy Mason Memorial is a small park designed by landscape architects Katherine Spitz and Pamela Burton, perfect for catching a bit of shade and learning some history. Beyond the trees and benches, you'll find the centerpiece of the park, an 80-foot-long concrete wall by artist Sheila Levrant de Bretteville. The wall features a timeline of Mason's life with embedded plaques and carved impressions of objects from throughout her life, including wagon wheels, a midwife's bag, and the deed to her homestead.

THE BROWN DERBY

Where can you find the hat-shaped dome of what was one of the most famous restaurants in the world?

It takes a bit of hunting, but once you spot it hiding on the roof of a Koreatown strip mall, there's no mistaking the signature shape of the legendary Brown Derby restaurant. While these days the crowds line up nearby for Korean BBQ and spicy crab, this giant bowler hat was once a favorite destination of the who's who of Hollywood.

Originally constructed in 1926 as a small cafe at 3427 Wilshire Blvd., the 32-by-33-foot hat was rebuilt a half block east at Alexandria in 1937 with an expanded dining room and patio, and topped by a neon sign that read "Eat in the Hat." Legend has it that the restaurant began as a dare when screenwriter Wilson Mizner challenged movie producer Herbert Somborn (Gloria Swanson's second husband), saying "If you know anything about food, you can sell it out of a hat." Together, along with theater impresario Sid Grauman, they opened The Little Hat, which was soon renamed The Brown Derby (some say after a Long Island restaurant popular with vaudeville actors).

From the start, the restaurant was a magnet for Hollywood stars—including Will Rogers, Mary Pickford, and Charlie Chaplin—thanks in part to its proximity to the famed and now long-gone Ambassador Hotel and its tropical themed Cocoanut Grove nightclub. Following the success of the first Derby, a second location opened at Hollywood and Vine on Valentine's Day, 1929.

THE BROWN DERBY

What: A hat-shaped icon from the Golden Era of Hollywood

Where: 3377 Wilshire Blvd.

Cost: Free

Pro Tip: You can still find the neon sign from the Hollywood Brown Derby at the Museum of Neon Art in Glendale, and you can dine at a recreation of that location at Disney World.

The hat-shaped Brown Derby was one of the more famous examples of programmatic or mimetic architecture. These whimsical and wacky buildings were designed to catch the eye of passing motorists and could be found all over Southern California, often resembling what they sold, including donuts, hot dogs, cameras, or other objects. Photo by Danny Jensen.

Additional locations were built in Beverly Hills and Los Feliz, and were popular destinations for decades, but by the mid-1980s, all four locations were shuttered. In 1985, the original hat-shaped building and brim were moved and eventually placed on the third floor of a shiny new shopping plaza—known as Brown Derby Plaza—built on the site of the former restaurant. It's there where you can still tip your hat to the remnants of a Hollywood icon that currently sits unoccupied.

While not shaped like a hat, the Hollywood location was understandably even more star-studded and a favorite hangout of Lucille Ball, Jack Benny, Clark Gable (who supposedly proposed to Carole Lombard there), and many more celebrities whose faces also lined the walls as caricatures. It's also where co-owner Robert Cobb first created the Cobb salad, allegedly by throwing together ingredients from the fridge for friends.

HOLYLAND EXHIBITION

Where can you find artifacts from the Middle East gathered by a real life Indiana Jones?

In the hills of Silver Lake stands a hidden museum dedicated to Antonia Futterer, an Australian-born explorer, evangelist, and lecturer who went in search of the Ark of the Covenant, the sacred chest thought to hold the tablets engraved with the Ten Commandments. Sound familiar? Thought to be one of the real-world inspirations for Indiana Jones, Futterer may not have found the Ark, but he did bring back a wealth of artifacts from the Middle East that can now be explored at his former home by appointment.

Looking up at the Spanish Colonial Revival–style home on an out-of-the-way residential street, you'd have a hard time distinguishing the museum from other homes in the neighborhood—were it not for a small sign in the window that reads, "Holyland Exhibition." But once inside, the difference is immediately clear as you're led on a roughly two-hour guided tour that features five rooms filled floor to ceiling with artifacts, furniture, tapestries, photographs, and more collected from Egypt, Palestine, Syria, and elsewhere in the region.

Born in Australia in 1871, Futterer spent his early years in the family business of weaving cane furniture before venturing west in hopes of striking it rich in the outback during the 1890s gold rush. But instead of great fortune, Futterer found himself battling appendicitis. Faced with the prospect of death, Futterer made a pact

During the tour, you'll encounter a life-size sculpture of Jesus praying by a large rock, which older Angelenos may remember from the meditation room of the long-gone Clifton's Silver Spoon Cafeteria. Clifford E. Clinton's son donated the statue to the museum, along with a 2,000-year-old Phoenician glass vial used for eyeliner.

Standouts from the collection include a 2,700-year-old sarcophagus, 5,000-year-old oil lamps, an ornately designed ancient game table from Damascus, and Futterer's "Eye-Ographic Bible," which includes colored slides and maps that he used in his lectures. Photo by Adrienne Florez.

HOLYLAND EXHIBITION

What: The home-turned-museum of an early 20th-century explorer

Where: 2213 Lake View Ave.

Cost: Suggested donation of $2.50 for adults, $2 for children

Pro Tip: The museum is open year-round by appointment only, so be sure to call first: (323) 664-3162.

with God—despite not having a religious upbringing—that if he survived, he would dedicate his life to teaching the bible. When he recovered, he set about fulfilling his promise, preaching throughout the region before being sent, along with his wife, to Oakland in 1911 by evangelist Alexis Jeffries.

In 1924, Futterer moved to LA, where he started a mission Downtown LA; later in Silver Lake, he opened the Holyland Bible Knowledge Society, which offered classes to people of all faiths and nonbelievers alike. Soon after, he went looking for the Ark, which he believed was hidden beneath Mt. Nebo in modern-day Jordan. And while local authorities didn't allow Futterer to explore his theory fully, he did manage to acquire a bewilderingly large collection of items from the region, all of which are now on display at the Holyland Exhibition.

Even if you don't consider yourself religious, the Holyland Exhibition is a fascinating museum to explore, filled to the brim with historic and cultural artifacts. It's also a compelling look at the life of a passionate collector. Although Futterer passed away in 1949, his followers have maintained the collection and lead the tours.

ST. VINCENT COURT

Where can you grab a bite to eat on the hidden site of LA's first college?

Walking down 7th Street between Broadway and Hill Street in Downtown LA, you might think you've stumbled upon a movie studio backlot as you look down an alleyway lined with colorful, European-style restaurant facades, faux balconies, and cafe tables on the sidewalk. Instead, you've found St. Vincent Court—an under-the-radar lunch destination and the site of LA's first institution of higher learning.

Founded by Thaddeus Amat, Southern California's first bishop and a member of the Vincentian Order, St. Vincent's College first opened in 1865 at the corner of Los Angeles and Alameda Streets. While what we consider a college has changed quite a bit since then, St. Vincent's is regarded as the city's first post-high school educational institution—three years before the University of California system and 15 years before USC was founded.

In 1867, the college relocated to a new campus on a 10-acre plot bounded by Broadway, Olive, 6th Street, and Eighth Street. At the center of the campus was St. Vincent's Place, a 40-foot wide and 480-foot long carriageway. The school remained there until relocating again in 1887, eventually merging with Loyola College, which would later become Loyola Marymount University.

ST. VINCENT COURT

What: A historic courtyard with European-inspired facades and good eats

Where: Off 7th Street between Hill Street and Broadway

Cost: Free, except for the food

Pro Tip: Be sure to head around the corner on Broadway to visit Clifton's Cafeteria, another legendary LA landmark, for a bite and visit one of their numerous bars.

While many of Downtown LA's alleyways don't offer much to look at, there's one that promises not only a colorful slice of the city's history but also a great bite to eat. Photo by Danny Jensen.

While the school may have moved on, the carriageway of St. Vincent's Place would become a permanent fixture of Downtown LA, thanks to the opening of the first Bullock's department store in 1907. The palatial department store used St. Vincent's Place for deliveries and added walkways above the passage to connect the buildings on either side.

In 1957, Bullocks added some charm to the passageway with retail shops and cafes, along with European-inspired plaster facades, faux balconies with figurines, and herringbone brick on the ground. The first tenants of the newly renamed St. Vincent's Court included a flower shop, a newsstand, a bookstore, and Ambrose Pasquini's Espresso Bar—thought to be the first of its kind in the neighborhood.

After the original Bullocks closed in 1983, the buildings were renovated to become the Saint Vincent Jewelry Center, featuring wholesale and retail jewelry sellers. As the neighborhood shifted from the once-bustling upscale shopping destination to the Jewelry District, many of the businesses of St. Vincent's Court likewise changed. Thankfully, the kitschy facades have remained, and now hungry shoppers can grab delicious spit-roasted meats and other Turkish specialties at the Sevan Garden Kebab House, Persian dishes at Farid Restaurant, Armenian fare and slices at Pizza Italia—and an espresso at Le Cafe Bonjour.

While the city recently cracked down on outdoor seating that had occupied the center of the alley for decades, you can still dine al fresco on small sidewalk tables and feel as though you're traveling in the Old World, far from LA.

OUTER LIMITS TATTOO

Where can you get inked at the oldest tattoo parlor in the United States?

If you're getting a tattoo, it's probably a safe bet to go to a place where they've been putting ink to skin for nearly a century. That being said, there's no better destination than Outer Limits Tattoo in Long Beach—considered the oldest continually operating tattoo parlor in the United States and the second (or third, depending on who you ask) oldest in the world. Even if you never plan on getting inked, Outer Limits is worth a visit to learn the history of the art and the colorful personalities behind it.

Located on the basement level of the historic Sovereign Building, the storefront first opened in 1921 as a photography studio. Then in 1927, a tattoo parlor took over, and while many of the early details are lost, it's believed to have been known as The Professionals. At the time, the area surrounding the shop was a raucous seaside amusement park known as the Pike. Starting in 1919, Long Beach became the homeport to the US Navy's Pacific Fleet, and the Pike—and its many tattoo parlors—became a popular destination for sailors on shore leave.

Around 1954, legendary tattoo artist Bert Grimm opened Bert Grimm's World Famous Tattoo Studio in the Sovereign Building's space. Grimm is considered one of the pioneers of the American Traditional style of tattooing—big, bold black outlines, a limited number of bright colors, and now-iconic tattoos: bald eagles, snakes, nautical themes, and pinup girls.

Among the more unusual discoveries made during the renovations in 2002 was a giant drum barrel half full of petroleum jelly once used for tattooing, a vintage cash register, and a huge safe found behind a false wall. Despite curiosity, the safe remains unopened.

While renovating the shop, which included revealing the original flooring, Kari Barba and her team uncovered a treasure trove of memorabilia, including a window that was hand-painted by Bob Shaw with tattoo designs. Photo by Danny Jensen.

OUTER LIMITS TATTOO

What: The oldest continually operating tattoo parlor in the United States

Where: 22 S. Chestnut Pl., Long Beach

Cost: Free, unless you're getting a tattoo, of course

Pro Tip: Try visiting during a weekday, when the shop is a bit quieter, and politely ask if someone can show you around.

Grimm, along with his wife Julie, would go on to open more tattoo shops in the Long Beach area (as well as in San Diego and Portland, Oregon). Bert Grimm also became a mentor to other influential tattoo artists such as Lyle Tuttle and Bob Shaw. Shaw would eventually buy Grimm's tattoo parlors, and the Shaw family would run them in the decades to follow. Then, in 2002, Shaw's sons planned to close the historic Long Beach shop, but before the space could disappear into obscurity, tattoo artist Kari Barba bought it and reopened it as Outer Limits Tattoo.

Barba painstakingly tracked down and organized photographs and artifacts from the history of the legendary tattoo parlor, creating a small museum. Glass cases showcase vintage tattoo machines and flash sheets of decades-old tattoo designs, while photos on the wall feature tattoo artists, customers, and images of the Pike over the years. It's a fascinating glimpse at how the area has evolved and a testament to the spirit that has persisted in the shop.

THE SANTA MONICA MOSAIC HOUSE

Where can you find a home that's covered in tile mosaics?

Along 26th Street in Santa Monica, there's one house that stands out from the rest of the charming homes: a 1930s bungalow that's completely covered in colorful and detailed mosaics designs made of broken tiles, plates, glass, and more. The Santa Monica Mosaic House, home to Louise and Aziz Farnham, is worth a visit to admire the stunning and unique artwork that's taken years to create.

The story of the Mosaic House began when Louise volunteered to help create small mosaics with one of her son's fourth grade class to sell at a Halloween fundraiser. A midwife by trade in her native Iran before she was forced to flee in 1981 after the Iranian Revolution, Louise had long had a talent for needlepoint and creating handmade blankets and baskets. But after her first experience with mosaics, she was immediately hooked. She promptly took to decorating a table lamp with faux pearls and fragments of rose-patterned plates. She soon moved to new projects, covering bowls, vases, and entire coffee tables with pieces of china, tile, mirror, and other vibrant artifacts. The centerpiece of the home is the living room fireplace, spectacularly adorned with pieces of mirror from floor to ceiling.

While Aziz wasn't initially enthusiastic about his wife's new artistic endeavor, he soon had a change of heart when another one of their

THE SANTA MONICA MOSAIC HOUSE

What: A colorful home covered with mosaic tilework

Where: 2525 California Ave., Santa Monica

Cost: Free

Pro Tip: To purchase some of Louise's incredible mosaic artwork or to commission a piece, be sure to visit her website: https://www.custommosaicart.com.

sons encouraged his father to add tiles to a concrete retaining wall in front of the home. Aziz soon caught the mosaic bug himself, and together with Louise began collecting plates, tiles, figurines, marble, and more from thrift stores, gift shops, flea markets, and elsewhere to use for their creations.

Aziz began decorating the exterior of the house in 2000, adding sections over time with some taking a few months and others an entire year of whatever spare time he had. The exterior designs include an eclectic and vivid array of themes, everything from grape vines and fruit trees, to a giant killer whale and a river full of fish that runs along the entire length of the house.

By 2014, the entire exterior of the Farnham's house was covered in mosaic designs. The couple estimates that for both the interior pieces and the exterior work, they've used more than 25 million pieces. Highlights of the exterior include a depiction of the Hollywood sign that faces the alleyway, a unicorn, and colorful exotic birds inspired by the family's real-life pets.

The Farnham's Mosaic House has drawn visitors from all over the world, including fellow artists looking for inspiration. While it's a private home, most of the exterior mosaics can easily be seen from the street without disturbing the family—though they have been known to welcome in the occasional polite visitor.

If you're looking for other impressive displays of mosaic artwork, be sure to visit the Watts Towers by Simon Rodia and the Mosaic Tile House of Venice.

THE THEME BUILDING AT LAX

What's up with that space-age structure in the middle of LAX?

Amid the chaos of arriving at Los Angeles International Airport, countless visitors—and younger Angelenos—have likely looked up at the soaring arches and mysterious spaceship-like structure of the Theme Building in the center of the airport's terminals and wondered, "What the heck is that thing?" An iconic yet often overlooked symbol of the city and a masterpiece of mid-century modern architecture, the futuristic-looking building is mostly out of commission, but it could become a hub of activity again sometime in the future.

Completed in 1961, the Theme Building features two enormous parabolic arches of stucco-covered steel connected by a circular structure that appears to be floating like a flying saucer. Often mistaken for an air traffic control tower, the saucer housed an 8,000-square-foot restaurant with floor-to-ceiling windows and an observation deck on the roof. A silo-shaped tower rising up through the center of the building would shuttle visitors to the restaurant and deck. The $2.2-million structure was developed through the partnership of three major architectural firms—Pereira & Luckman and Associates, Welton Becket and Associates, and Paul R. Williams—and the design was directed by architect Gin Wong. Wong also played a major role in designing other LA landmarks, including LACMA and the cube of CBS Television City.

The original design for the Theme Building included a massive glass dome that would cover the structure and connect it to surrounding terminals and parking.

The Theme Building is thought to be a major design influence for the space-age world of The Jetsons. Photo by Danny Jensen.

THE THEME BUILDING AT LAX

What: An iconic mid-century structure that looks straight out of *The Jetsons*

Where: 201 World Way

Cost: Free

Pro Tip: Park on the rooftop of the temporary parking structures 2A or 6 for great views of the Theme Building.

While the Theme Building was once a symbol of the modern Jet Age and of a time when air travel was more leisurely and stylish, it experienced several setbacks over the years. Following 9/11, the observation deck was temporarily closed. While it eventually reopened, tighter security made the building less popular. Then, in 2007, a half-ton piece of stucco fell from one of the arches and broke apart on the rooftop, leading to a three-year, $14 million renovation and seismic retrofit. In 2014, the building's restaurant, Encounters, closed for good, and the observation deck closed in 2018.

But worry not space-age travelers, there may come a day soon when the Theme Building will once again play a starring role at LAX. The Bob Hope USO recently opened on the ground floor of the building for military service members and their families. And the airport is now considering design proposals for the Theme Building as part of a major modernization and expansion project that will include an elevated people-mover train planned for 2023. Initial talk suggests the building could be used as a restaurant, museum, or meeting space. In the meantime, we can still admire the inspirational design of the mid-century marvel.

BALLERINA CLOWN

Why is there a giant clown dancing in Venice?

Venice is home to plenty of eccentric street performers, but there are few that can command quite as much attention as the 30-foot-tall bearded clown in a tutu, gracefully balanced on a soapbox above the entrance to a mixed-use building at the corner of Rose Avenue and Main Street. The massive, head-turning sculpture, known as *Ballerina Clown*, was created by the artist Jonathan Borofsky. And while the classical clown was designed to kick its right leg as part of a perpetual dance, more often than not the sculpture has remained motionless, poised in the spotlight.

Commissioned by developer Harlan Lee and installed in 1989, *Ballerina Clown* sports Depression-era hobo clown makeup, and is stylishly, if peculiarly, clad in a gray tutu and blue top with white gloves and matching red pointed shoes and top hat. Made of aluminum, steel, and painted fiberglass, the sculpture also contains a motor to swing its right leg.

Unfortunately, not everyone appreciated the clown's graceful dance. Not long after it was installed, the swinging leg came to a halt after neighbors in the building complained about the mechanical noise. A mere 25 years later, the mechanical issues were fixed and

> ### BALLERINA CLOWN
>
> **What:** A giant dancing clown
>
> **Where:** Main Street and Rose Avenue
>
> **Cost:** Free
>
> **Pro Tip:** Stand on the southeast corner of the intersection to enjoy the best view of the *Ballerina Clown*.

Another *Ballerina Clown* by Borofsky can be found in the courtyard of the Ludwig Forum for International Art in Aachen, Germany, where it was installed in 1991.

66

"The Venice Boardwalk is full of all kinds of people in all sorts of outfits, and the atmosphere is very festive with many live street performances taking place, especially on weekends. This sculpture is an accommodation or resolution of opposites in one," explained Jonathan Borofsky in a statement about Ballerina Clown. *"Not only does this image bring the male and female together into one figure, but also, two opposite types of performers are represented: the formal classical ballet dancer and the traditional street performer. Of course, this public sculpture might push the envelope in 'taste,' but if you have ever walked the Venice Boardwalk on a Sunday afternoon, you might understand why this figure is right at home." Photo by Danny Jensen.*

approvals were given to allow *Ballerina Clown* to dance once again—if only during the day. The leg is scheduled to kick daily from 1 p.m. to 6 p.m., but even if you don't catch the performance, *Ballerina Clown* is still worth a visit.

67

A BREWERY'S BATCHELDER TILES

Where can you grab a beer and find historic tiles made by a legendary craftsman?

While brewery taprooms are often barebones warehouses, one purveyor of craft suds in the Arts District defies the norm. At Angel City Brewery, you'll not only find a historic factory where bridge cables were once made but also tiles by Ernest Batchelder, LA's most iconic tile artists of the Craftsman period—if you know where to look.

Built in 1913, the brewery's 69,000-square-foot home was originally a warehouse for the John A. Roebling's Sons Company, which manufactured "wire rope" used to suspend the Brooklyn Bridge, the Golden Gate Bridge, and LA Harbor's Vincent Thomas Bridge. The company also produced power lines for LA and metal for Slinkys! Inside Angel City Brewery, you'll see an imposing iron slide spiraling up to the ceiling that was once used to roll huge, 800-pound spools of wire rope down to the loading docks.

While the entrance to Angel City Brewery is on Traction Avenue, if you follow directions to 216 Alameda St., you'll encounter a set of locked double doors. Peering inside, you'll spy the former office lobby of John A. Roebling's Sons, featuring a stained-glass chandelier, a mosaic floor with the initials J. A. R., and, most notably, decorative terra-cotta tiles along the brick walls created by Batchelder. Other

---

A BREWERY'S BATCHELDER TILES

What: Famous Batchelder tiles hidden inside a brewery

Where: 216 Alameda St.

Cost: Free

Pro Tip: Check the Angel City Brewery website for fun weekly activities such as trivia, comedy, and yoga. And don't miss the daily tours of the brewery, which include a tasting.

To design his tiles, Batchelder used the distinctive method known as "engobe," in which the design would be hand-carved and then painted over with wet clay, with the excess wiped away before firing. Photo by Danny Jensen.

works by the famous Pasadena-based tile maker can be found surrounding the fireplaces and fountains of historic Craftsman homes throughout LA and beyond.

The intricately designed, custom Batchelder tiles were gifted to the John A. Roebling's Sons Company by its employees, according to one of the tiles above a beautiful square tile of two peacocks. The collection of 44-tile collection depicts the life and work of John A. Roebling, who emigrated from Prussia to New Jersey with dreams of creating a "technological utopia." You'll see the boat he arrived on, the 1848 workshop where he developed the wire rope that would innovate bridge building, examples of the rope in action, and one of his crowning achievements, the Brooklyn Bridge.

While the lobby isn't typically open to the public, the brewery does offer periodic art tours that include a visit to the room, along with a guided tour of the modern murals that now surround the building—offering a great contrast of artistic styles.

Batchelder tiles can also be found in the El Dorado Lofts on Spring Street (though some say most are replicas) and the Fine Arts Building on 7th Street. One of the most impressive collections is sadly off-limits to the public in what was once the Dutch Chocolate Shop on 6th Street by Spring, which features huge, custom-designed murals of daily life in Holland.

FERNDELL NATURE MUSEUM

Where in Griffith Park can you escape to a tropical oasis?

Covering more than 4,000 acres, Griffith Park is one of the country's largest urban parks (five times as big as New York's Central Park) and is full of plenty of wonderful places to explore. But while most people are familiar with its sun-drenched hiking trails, the iconic Hollywood sign, the observatory, the zoos (both the abandoned and the new), and other landmarks, the park also offers a peaceful and shady, stream-lined trail that is often overlooked.

The Ferndell (also spelled Fern Dell) Nature Museum isn't a museum in the typical sense with four walls, but rather a canopied, quarter-mile canyon teeming with wildlife and perfect for cooling off on a hot day. You'll find the entrance to the trail at the southwest corner of Griffith Park, about 450 feet up Fern Dell Drive on the left, just up the hill from the Los Feliz Boulevard entrance with the statue of the waving bear cub.

Originally known as Mococahuenga by the native Gabrielino-Tongva people who used the area for tribal meetings, the canyon was first planted with native and imported ferns around 1912 by Frank Shearer, the Los Angeles Superintendent of Parks at the time. Rustic bridges, terraced pools, and footpaths were added in the 1920s. During the Great Depression, workers and artisans from the Civilian Conservation Corps expanded Ferndell, adding stone walls, water features, terraced areas with benches, and concrete railings carved to look like wood. By the 1980s, the area had fallen into disrepair, but thanks to ongoing restoration efforts by the Griffith Park Historic Fern Dell Preservation Project, Ferndell is gradually being restored to its former glory.

In the 1920s, Ferndell became a popular destination for health-seekers as the canyon's natural spring was thought to have restorative powers—it was even nicknamed the Fountain of Youth.

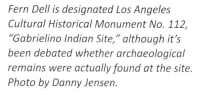

Fern Dell is designated Los Angeles Cultural Historical Monument No. 112, "Gabrielino Indian Site," although it's been debated whether archaeological remains were actually found at the site. Photo by Danny Jensen.

FERNDELL NATURE MUSEUM

What: A lush oasis hidden in Griffith Park

Where: 5375 Red Oak Drive at Fern Dell Drive

Cost: Free

Pro Tip: At the top of the Ferndell pathway, head left to find the Trails cafe, a charming spot with outdoor seating for light sandwiches, pastries, coffee, lemonade, and more.

If you're looking for a peaceful retreat from the city, especially when other parts of Griffith Park are hot and dry in the summer, strolling up the meandering gravel pathways of Ferndell is the perfect escape. As you walk or relax on a bench, keep an eye out for a mix of native and non-native ferns, including button, snail, and leatherleaf, as well as giant, tropical Elephant-ear plants that look straight out of *Jurassic Park*. Enjoy shade from a variety of trees, including western sycamore, native coast live oak, and California coastal redwoods. Peer into the ponds along the stream to see red-eared slider turtles, crayfish, goldfish, and snails, and watch for woodpeckers, hawks, rabbits, reptiles, and more.

71

THE COCA-COLA OCEANLINER

Why does it look like an ocean liner ran aground in the middle of Downtown LA?

Driving down the stretch of Central Avenue just north of the 10 freeway, there's not much to look at besides nondescript warehouses and parking lots. But if you're paying attention, you'll spot an enormous, Streamline Moderne ocean liner–shaped building that looks to be sailing down the avenue. It also happens to be where they bottle some of the Coca-Cola that Angelenos drink.

The Coca-Cola company first began operating in LA in 1902, setting up shop not too far away at Third and Los Angeles Streets with a humble two-man operation. The company moved a few more times before docking on Central Avenue. The facility eventually expanded to four buildings, which included bottling, warehouses, and offices. Then, in 1936, Stanley Barbee, president of the Coca-Cola Bottling Co. of Southern California, hired architect Robert V. Derrah to turn the four buildings into one. That same year, Derrah had just completed Crossroads of the World in Hollywood, a shopping center that resembles a Streamline Moderne ship. Barbee, a boating enthusiast himself, thought a similar ship theme for the bottling plant would, according to the Los Angeles Times, "project the attributes Coca-Cola sought to promote: modernity, cleanliness and progress."

THE COCA-COLA OCEANLINER

What: A bottling plant made to look like a Streamline Moderne ocean liner

Where: 1334 South Central Ave.

Cost: Free

Pro Tip: Across the street from the ocean liner, check out the African American Firefighters Museum, open Sunday, Tuesday, and Thursday afternoons.

The building was declared one of LA's historic-cultural monuments in 1976, and while the property has expanded to occupy huge warehouses behind the ocean liner, they still keep the facade in ship shape.

Completed in 1939, the Derrah-designed ocean liner spans an entire block of Central Avenue and wraps around onto 14th Street with two levels of portal windows, rivets made of wood, and a promenade deck running along the second level. The "vessel" is primarily white with a black bottom, and the distinctive Coca-Cola red runs in between and adorns the ship's bridge in the company's familiar font. It's an impressive sight to behold. And while unfortunately, they don't allow tours, the nautical theme reportedly continues inside with mahogany decks, railings, doors with portholes, and ventilators once used as chutes for bottle caps. As you stroll around the exterior of the building, don't miss the giant terracotta Coke bottles at the corners of the building across 14th Street.

You can spot the signature Coca-Cola font etched above the entrance of another building not far away at the corner of 4th and Merrick Streets. Built in 1915, the three-story building was used to produce syrup using the company's secret formula and was recently converted into upscale offices.

NEON RETRO ARCADE

Where can you play classic arcade games without blowing all your laundry money?

If you spent any amount of time mashing buttons on pinball machines and video games at arcades and pizza parlors as a kid, then you're bound to lose a few hours at Neon Retro Arcade—without having to worry about greasy buttons and sticky floors. And while bars with vintage arcade games have become increasingly popular, this is one place where players of all ages can aim to beat the high score.

Husband-and-wife team Mark Guenther and Mia Mazadiego first opened Neon Retro Arcade in Pasadena in 2015, featuring games that grew out of a personal collection. The 2,000-square foot space features a well-curated and well-maintained selection of over 40 full-sized arcade games and pinball machines, featuring classic titles from the '80s and '90s as well as some hard-to-find games.

And perhaps best of all, rather than having to drop quarter after quarter into the machines, you'll pay just $15 per hour for

NEON RETRO ARCADE

What: Classic arcade games and pinball machines available for all ages

Where: 28 S. Raymond Ave., Pasadena

Cost: $15 per hour or $25 for an all-day pass

Pro Tip: You can fuel up with snacks, soda, and water available at the front; there are also several nearby restaurants.

If you're looking to bring the arcade experience home, check out the Vintage Arcade Superstore in Glendale where you can buy and rent arcade games and pinball machines.

While the games can rotate, you'll find everything from Asteroids and Donkey Kong to Mortal Kombat and The Simpsons, and for pinball, you'll find the classic Twilight Zone alongside the new Star Trek. At the back of the arcade, you'll find screens connected to home consoles with newer games. Photo by Danny Jensen.

unlimited game play or $25 to play all day. You can rent out the arcade for birthdays or private events, and the arcades often hosts fundraisers for local charities and schools.

CAPITOL RECORDS MORSE CODE

Is the Capitol Records Building sending out a secret message?

Resembling a stack of records on a turntable, the Capitol Records Building is an instantly recognizable Hollywood icon, towering a block north of the intersection of Hollywood and Vine. But most people don't realize that the blinking light atop the circular building's 90-foot rooftop spire has been sending out a secret message for decades—unless of course you're a very observant reader of Morse code.

To promote Capitol Records' status as the first record label with a West Coast home, then-president Alan Livingston decided that the red light at the top of the building's spire should continuously blink the word "Hollywood" in Morse code. To commemorate the occasion, they even invited Leila Morse, the granddaughter of Samuel Morse, to throw the switch. The message has continued to flicker out into the night to this day with only a couple of exceptions. To celebrate the label's 50th anniversary the message was changed to "Capitol 50" for a year, beginning in June 1992. Oddly, the only other time it was changed was to promote a Katy Perry album for a few months, flashing out, "Katy Perry. Prism. October 22, 2013." Maybe they'll find another reason in the future.

During the holiday season, the roof of the Capitol Records Building also features a Christmas tree made of 4,373 bulbs. The tree has made an appearance every December since 1958 except in 1973 (due to an energy crisis). (Photo by Adrienne Florez)

Designed by Louis Naidorf of Welton Becket Associates, the 13-story tower was the world's first circular office building when it was completed in 1956. Naidorf insists that he didn't intend for the building to look like a stack of records, and was only told that it was to be used for "Project X"—the codename for the company's venture.

THE GREAT LOS ANGELES AIR RAID

Did mysterious enemy aircraft threaten LA during World War II, or was it an extraterrestrial visit?

Air raid sirens blaring. A barrage of bullets whizzing through the air. Searchlights panning the sky for an unseen enemy. The Great Los Angeles Air Raid of 1942—also known as the Battle of Los Angeles— may sound like the stuff of movies to most Angelenos these days, but the dramatic experience was very real to those living in LA on February 25, 1942—even if the supposed attack turned out to be an illusion. And for those curious to know what the experience was like, in true Hollywood fashion, you can now take part in an annual re-creation of that fateful night.

Following the attack on Pearl Harbor on December 7, 1941, Southern California and the rest of the country were on high alert, and mandatory blackouts and air raid drills were common. On February 23, the war came even closer to home when a Japanese submarine appeared in the waters just north of Santa Barbara and shelled Ellwood Oil Field (the damage was minimal and no lives were lost).

Then, at 2:25 a.m. on February 25, the US Army announced the approach of unidentified, hostile aircraft heading toward Los Angeles.

Many of the visitors to the re-creation of the air raid wear vintage 1940s dresses and military uniforms. Prior to the air raid simulation, the night includes big band music, swing dancing, dinner, and the chance to explore the museum and its rarely seen collection of military vehicles. It's an amazing evening for history lovers, veterans, and anyone curious about the historic night.

While some believe it may have been an errant weather balloon that showed up on radar and triggered the alarm, other theories—especially during the 1970s—suggest that it was extraterrestrial crafts that were spotted. We may never know. . . . Photo by Danny Jensen.

THE GREAT LOS ANGELES AIR RAID

What: A re-creation of a mysterious and terrifying night in LA history

Where: 3601 S. Gaffey St., San Pedro

Cost: $25 in advance, $40 at the gate

Pro Tip: While the air raid re-creation takes place only once a year in February, the Fort MacArthur Museum is worth a visit year round.

Suddenly, the night resounded with air raid sirens, searchlights lit up the sky, and heavy-duty anti-aircraft batteries, positioned around the region, began firing explosive charges into the night sky for nearly an hour. More than 1,400 rounds were fired, but not a single one hit enemy aircraft— because it seems there was no aircraft to be hit. While multiple eyewitness accounts insisted that they saw something, and some claimed they saw a V-shaped formation of planes, ultimately, no trace of enemy aircraft or troops was ever found. Sadly, there were five fatalities, but those were due to traffic accidents in the blackout and heart attacks. The Secretary of the Navy eventually had to admit that there were no enemy aircraft and that the "Battle of Los Angeles" was really a result of wartime jitters.

To commemorate the Great Los Angeles Air Raid, the Fort MacArthur Museum in San Pedro (which was active during the "battle") hosts an annual reenactment of the dramatic evening, complete with sirens and searchlights, simulated airplane sounds, and very real—and loud—firing of the fort's anti-aircraft guns (and fireworks for good measure).

HIGHLAND PARK BOWL

How was LA's oldest bowling alley brought back to life?

Originally opened in 1927, Highland Park Bowl has long been a beloved destination for bowling, live music, and cocktails. Thanks to a painstaking restoration, the nightlife spot was brought back to its former glory.

When Highland Park Bowl first opened, in the midst of Prohibition, savvy bowlers looking to imbibe would allegedly head upstairs to a doctor to obtain a prescription for "medicinal" whiskey. They could then fill those prescriptions at the pharmacy downstairs and make their way to the bowling lanes for a night of revelry.

In 1966, the bowling alley underwent a transformation under the new ownership of Joseph "Mr. T" Teresa, an Italian immigrant who renamed the destination Mr. T's Bowl. Dropped ceilings and paint obscured the building's original designs, and by the late '80s, the lanes were closed leaving just the bar. Years later, Mr. T's became a destination for up-and-coming bands, including everything from punk to hip hop. While Mr. T's continued to operate after Teresa passed away in 2003, many felt its time had come to an end. That is until the 1933 Group, known for operating vintage-inspired bars and restoring historic sites, stepped in.

The group's $2 million restoration revealed many of the spectacular details of Highland Park Bowl that had been hidden for decades, including a bow-truss ceiling with skylights and a beautiful Arts and

HIGHLAND PARK BOWL

What: A lovingly restored Prohibition-era bowling alley.

Where: 5621 N Figueroa St., Highland Park

Cost: Hourly lane prices range from $25-$70 depending on time and day. Shoe rentals are $5

Pro Tip: Check the Bowl's calendar to catch burlesque performances, live music, open mic nights, and more.

Layers of paint had covered a stunning Arts and Crafts mural of a forest painted by the Anderson Brothers in the 1930s across the entire back wall of the bowling alley.

Crafts mural along the back wall. Restored vintage pinsetters remain uncovered to reveal their inner workings while broken ones were converted into chandeliers. Other vintage finds were incorporated into the redesign, including pennants, photos, pins, and 70 cases of unopened liquor from 1972.

In addition to bowling LA's oldest lanes, visitors to Highland Park Bowl can now enjoy live music and performances, Neapolitan-style pizza, and a full bar with creative cocktails—no prescription needed.

The 1933 Group has also beautifully restored other iconic LA venues, including the giant whiskey-barrel-shaped Idle Hour, legendary Hollywood hangout The Formosa Café, and the beloved Tail o' the Pup hot dog stand.

LLANO DEL RIO

Where can you find the ruins of a once-thriving socialist colony?

Along the Pearblossom Freeway in northern LA County, lonely cobblestone chimneys mysteriously emerge from the desert landscape. These are the ghostly remains of the Llano del Rio Cooperative Colony, considered "the most important non-religious Utopian experiment in western American history," according to Knox Mellon, former head of California's Office of Historic Preservation.

Founded in 1914, Llano Del Rio was the vision of Job Harriman, a socialist lawyer who ran for vice president of the United States, California governor, and mayor of LA—a position he stood a chance of winning in 1911.

Following another failed mayoral run in 1913, Harriman set his sights on the Antelope Valley where he envisioned a model socialist colony, founded on cooperative economic ideals. Harriman, with five partners, purchased 9,000 acres of land near Big Rock Creek. Within the first year, 100 colonists began digging irrigation ditches and planting crops while living in tents.

One of the first structures built at Llano was a hotel and assembly hall—whose cobblestone chimneys and porch columns stand today. By 1917, the colony grew to nearly 900 members working within 60 departments, including a cannery, dairy, bakery, art studio, and school. Ongoing social activities, craft clubs, and dances kept the colonists entertained.

Despite the appearance of a thriving, nearly autonomous colony, Llano Del Rio faced numerous challenges. Infighting, lawsuits, attacks

In 1982, a 150-pound plaque designating Llano Del Rio as a California Historical Landmark was installed, but the sign was stolen two weeks later. Despite some fencing, efforts to protect the ruins have been unsuccessful.

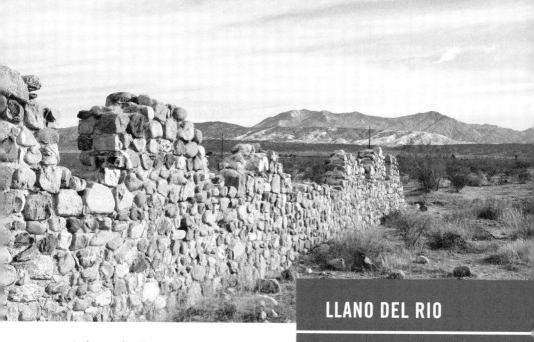

LLANO DEL RIO

Architect Alice Constance Austin proposed a "conscious feminist design" for Llano, a non-grid circular layout aimed at minimizing housework and to allow women to participate equally in governance and politics. However, the designs were never implemented.

What: The ruins of a long-abandoned socialist colony.

Where: Northside of Pearblossom Highway (CA 138), a half-mile east of 165th St. E

Cost: Free

Pro Tip: Stop for a photo at the intersection of CA 138 and 165th St. E, likely the location where David Hockney created his iconic "Pearblossom Highway" collage by taking over 800 photos of the landscape.

from the *Los Angeles Times*, financial woes, crop failures, and the inability to secure water rights eventually eroded its foundation. By the fall of 1917, Harriman and others relocated to a new site—a town in Louisiana renamed "New Llano." In 1918, Llano went into bankruptcy and the remaining colonists scattered, leaving the site to decay.

While Llano Del Rio may have been a fleeting experiment in American socialism, its ruins offer a reminder of what could have been an alternative path for Angelenos. In addition to seeing the chimneys up close, you can also wander around the crumbling stone walls and foundations of other buildings from this lost colony.

THE HOLLYHOCK HOUSE

Where can you tour an iconic Frank Lloyd Wright-designed home?

While the prairie-style homes designed by Frank Lloyd Wright in the Midwest receive plenty of attention, the legendary architect left a lasting impression on LA's landscape with buildings that took a dramatic stylistic departure, with designs that seemed inspired by Mayan, Egyptian, and Asian architecture. And while several of the Wright-designed homes in LA can be appreciated from the outside, there's only one that you can tour inside—the Hollyhock House in Los Feliz.

Situated atop what is now known as Barnsdall Art Park, the monumental Hollyhock House was built between 1919 and 1921 and was Wright's first LA commission. Designed for Aline Barnsdall, a wealthy oil heiress and patron of the arts, the 36-acre site was initially intended to serve as an elaborate complex of theaters, artist residences, and shops on top of Olive Hill for an avant-garde theater community. But due to artistic and financial differences (the project went way over budget), Barnsdall eventually fired Wright, and only three buildings were built—Hollyhock House and two guest houses. Barnsdall barely lived in the home before

THE HOLLYHOCK HOUSE

What: A Frank Lloyd Wright home that's open to the public

Where: 4800 Hollywood Blvd.

Cost: Self-guided tours are $7 for adults, $3 for seniors and students, and free for kids 12 and under. Docent-led exterior tours are an additional $7, and one-hour docent-led interior tours are $7 and offered Tuesdays and Wednesdays at 11 a.m. and 12:30 p.m.

Pro Tip: Check the Barnsdall Art Park website to find out about gallery exhibitions, theater performances, art classes, and Friday night wine tastings in the summer.

The style of the home is difficult to define—Wright himself described it as "California Romanza," from a musical term that he interpreted to mean "freedom to make one's own form"—though many see it as a bridge between his prairie-style homes and the textile block structures found elsewhere in LA (such as the famous Ennis House). Photo by Danny Jensen.

donating it to the City of Los Angeles in 1927 to be used as an art park in memory of her father, Theodore Barnsdall.

Time was not kind to the Hollyhock House, as it suffered damage from water, the 1994 Northridge earthquake, and several renovations that had mixed results. But after a meticulous four-year renovation that repaired damage, seismically retrofitted the structure, and restored historic elements, the home reopened to the public in 2015.

Now you can tour this stunning hilltop home, which was designed around Barnsdall's favorite flower, the Hollyhock, and seamlessly incorporates interior spaces with the outdoor landscape. While the exterior appears as an imposing monument of concrete almost like a Mayan temple, the interior feels lighter and more organic thanks to beautifully ornate woodwork and stained glass detailing. You can spot the Hollyhock flower motif throughout the building in furniture, art glass, and the ornamental cast concrete that runs along the exterior. And don't miss the incredible living-room hearth, a centerpiece for the home, which features a skylight above, a bas-relief stone mural, and a moat surrounding it (sadly, it's now dry due to the threat of water damage).

The Hollyhock House was recently designated a UNESCO World Heritage Site, along with seven other Wright-designed buildings across the country, and it's the first LA site to join the international list that includes Stonehenge and the Great Wall of China.

CALIFORNIA INSTITUTE OF ABNORMAL ARTS

Where can you see freak shows, punk bands, and the body of a dead French clown?

Nestled among the auto body shops of Burbank Boulevard in North Hollywood is a wildly surreal venue dedicated to all things strange, wonderfully weird, and, well, abnormal. The California Institute of Abnormal Arts—CIA for short, though none would confuse it for the other CIA—is the place to go if you're in search of performance art, costumed punk shows, magic, comedy, bizarre sideshow memorabilia, and other oddities.

Founded by Carl Crew, known as the "Barnham of Burbank Boulevard," along with his partner Robert Ferguson (both former embalmers at an LA mortuary), the location was originally intended to house the duo's film distribution company. When the venture failed, they began using the space to throw wild parties to keep the lights on, operating a speakeasy-style performance venue in the 1990s until it was shut down by the police. But since the show must go on, the pair eventually reopened the venue in 2001, this time with the necessary permits to host performers and serve beer and wine, and with an aesthetic and spirit inspired by the sideshow stages of traveling circuses of yore.

After you purchase your ticket—through the ear of a giant half-head/half-skull sculpture—you'll enter a courtyard that features a "Chinatown Circus" theme, with red lanterns strung up overhead and unusual artifacts lining the wall. In fact, nearly every corner of the CIA (which is laid out like a maze) is adorned with

Don't miss one of the CIA's wildest attractions: the embalmed body of a supposedly 100-year-old French clown.

Carl Crew, CIA co-founder, also wrote, produced, and starred in The Secret Life: Jeffrey Dahmer. *Photo courtesy California Institute of Abnormal Arts.*

CALIFORNIA INSTITUTE OF ABNORMAL ARTS

What: An offbeat venue for music, comedy, sideshow performers, and more

Where: 11334 Burbank Blvd., North Hollywood

Cost: Varies, but typically $10 cover

Pro Tip: Check the CIA's Facebook page for details on upcoming shows.

something that's bound to catch your eye, including skulls and shrunken heads, clowns, and cryptozoological displays. You can grab a drink at the bar to get your bearings, and depending on the night, catch a performance on the outside stage (perhaps a fire-eater or banjo-player), watch a B-movie on the outdoor screen (both Crew and Ferguson worked in the film industry), or head inside to the main stage where you can catch a wide range of acts, including macabre or oddly costumed punk acts, offbeat comedy, burlesque, and freak show performers—a little something for everyone—if you're open to the unusual.

THE BRUCE LEE STATUE (page 180)

THE LOTUS FESTIVAL (page 162)

THE MYSTIC MUSEUM (page 8)

THE *TRIFORIUM* (page 2)

THE THEME BUILDING AT LAX (page 64)

THE WITCH'S HOUSE (page 132)

THE PINK MOTEL (page 158)

THE WAYFARERS CHAPEL (page 176)

THE SANTA MONICA MOSAIC HOUSE (page 62)

BALLERINA CLOWN (page 66)

CHICKEN BOY (page 6)

THE HOLLYWOOD HERITAGE MUSEUM (page 140)

ANGELES CREST CREAMERY (page 4)

THE VICTORIANS OF CARROLL AVENUE (page 108)

OUTER LIMITS TATTOO (page 60)

ROUTE 66: END OF THE TRAIL

Why does America's most iconic highway end on an oceanside pier?

When you think of Route 66, aka the "Mother Road," you might picture classic convertibles cruising down the open road, passing kitschy motels, vintage gas stations, and retro burger stands, heading from frosty Chicago to the sunshine of Southern California. What you probably don't imagine is that if you continued following that iconic road to its westernmost point, you might find yourself careening off the Santa Monica Pier into the Pacific. In fact, many younger Angelenos may not even realize that the legendary route passes right through LA.

But Route 66 didn't always stretch quite so far west. Officially dedicated in 1926, the original terminus of the nearly 2,500 mile stretch of roadway was right in the heart of Downtown LA at the intersection of 7th Street and Broadway. The end of the line was then extended in 1936 to Santa Monica, but only as far as Lincoln and Olympic boulevards, and it remained there for decades to come, until Route 66 was decommissioned in 1985.

Then, capitalizing on renewed nostalgia for the "Main Street of America," the Route 66 Alliance partnered with the Santa Monica Pier Restoration Corporation and the Santa Monica Convention and

ROUTE 66: END OF THE TRAIL

What: The unofficial end of the Mother Road

Where: 330 Santa Monica Pier

Cost: Free

Pro Tip: During the summer, check out Twilight on the Pier, a free weekly music festival on the Santa Monica Pier that also includes comedy, art, food, and a beer and wine garden.

If you need some Route 66 souvenirs (or bait and tackle), be sure to head to the Last Stop Shop at the end of the pier. Photo by Danny Jensen.

Visitors Bureau, and the end of the trail was stretched out to the pier in 2009—just in time for the centennial anniversary of the pier. So, while it may not be the "official" end of the original route, the ocean views are certainly more scenic than the gridlock of Lincoln and Olympic.

Today you can find the "Route 66: End of Trail" sign toward the beginning of the Santa Monica Pier, just past the Bubba Gump Shrimp Co. Sure, it's a touristy area, but it's worth a visit for the Americana charm.

To continue the nostalgic trip, head to the intersection of Lincoln and Olympic boulevards to eat at Mel's Drive-in, which restored the Googie-style building that once housed the Penguin Coffee Shop.

THE VICTORIANS OF CARROLL AVENUE

Was Michael Jackson's "Thriller" filmed on one of LA's most historic streets?

While hundreds of beautifully ornate Victorian-era homes once dotted LA, the vast majority of them were torn down in the name of progress. Thankfully, you can still find some of these stunning architectural jewels hidden in neighborhoods throughout LA. One of the best places to see a large collection of restored homes from the period is on Carroll Avenue in Angelino Heights, one of LA's first suburbs.

During the mid-1880s, Los Angeles experienced a massive land boom and population growth thanks to the completion of the transcontinental railroads. Amid the boom, the subdivision of Angelino Heights was promoted as a quiet suburban retreat atop a hill with beautiful views and just a short cable car ride away from Downtown LA. Dozens of spectacular homes sprung up in the neighborhood at the time, designed in the popular Queen Anne and Eastlake Victorian styles. Picture highly detailed wood trim, bold color schemes, wraparound porches, towers, and turrets, and you'll start to get the idea. While the popular "Painted Ladies" of San Francisco may come to mind, you're going to find much more architectural variety and incredible flourishes in Angelino Heights.

While around 50 Victorian homes and carriage houses dot the neighborhood, you'll find the biggest concentration of them, and some of the best preserved examples, along Carroll Avenue. Many

To enjoy more Victorian-era homes, head to the Heritage Square Museum in Montecito Heights, where you can tour the interiors and take part in special events inspired by the time period.

To improve views of the homes on Carroll Avenue, utility poles and overhead wiring were removed between 1998 and 2003, creating the first "scenic underground wiring district" in California. Photo by Danny Jensen.

THE VICTORIANS OF CARROLL AVENUE

What: Beautifully preserved Victorian-era homes hidden on a quiet street

Where: 1300 block of Carroll Avenue

Cost: Free

Pro Tip: On the first Saturday of every month, join the LA Conservancy for a more than two hour tour of Angelino Heights to learn more about the history and architecture ($12 for adults, $10 for Conservancy members and kids under 17).

of the homes fell into disrepair over the decades, but during the 1970s, the neighborhood experienced a renaissance as new owners meticulously restored the historic features of the homes. In 1976, the 1300 block was listed on the National Register of Historic Places, and in 1983, Angelino Heights was declared the city's first historic preservation overlay zone so that the neighborhood's buildings would be protected.

As you stroll along the street, chances are you might even recognize some of the homes, including the Sanders House at 1345 Carroll Ave., which was featured in the video for Michael Jackson's "Thriller," and the Innes House at 1329 from the TV series *Charmed*. And while the neighborhood has been used in film and TV (even as far back as the silent era when many stars lived in the neighborhood), it remains a secret to many Angelenos. As you walk around the neighborhood, you'll also notice other beautiful architectural styles, including Craftsman/California bungalows, Mission Revival, and Streamline Moderne.

LOOFF'S LITE-A-LINE

What the heck is a Lite-a-line? And who was Looff?

Even though it's considered California's oldest gaming establishment, mention of Looff's Lite-a-Line tends to evoke more mystery than history for many people. A one-of-a-kind game of skill, the Lite-a-Line is an unusual hybrid of bingo and pinball, offering players the chance to win some money and experience a bit of Long Beach history at the same time.

When it first opened in 1941, four miles south of its current location amid strip malls, the Lite-a-Line was one of the many games and attractions that drew huge crowds to the Long Beach Pike. At the time, the game was one of many housed beneath the dome of Looff's Hippodrome, previously home to a carousel built by Charles I. D. Looff that had been relocated. One of America's most famous carousel designers, Looff built and carved the horses for the first carousel at Coney Island in 1876 and went on to design carousels and other rides across the country.

LOOFF'S LITE-A-LINE

What: A one-of-a-kind game with plenty of history

Where: 2500 Long Beach Blvd., Long Beach

Cost: $1.25 per game

Pro Tip: First-time players get a few practice games; they'll come in handy.

In 1911, Looff moved his carousel operation to Long Beach, where he built the city's first hand-carved carousel and helped to develop the Pike into an entertainment destination. Charles's son Arthur carried on the family tradition after his father passed away in 1918, building one of the few enduring remnants from the Pike—the Lite-a-Line. After the Pike closed in 1979, the Lite-a-Line was one of the few old businesses that held on—until it couldn't. Fortunately, Charles's son-in-law Mike Cincola preserved the game and relocated it to the current location about four miles north.

Charles Looff not only created Long Beach's first carousel, but he also had a hand in developing numerous other rides and amusement parks across the country, including a carousel for the Santa Cruz boardwalk and the Santa Monica Pier—originally known as Looff's Pleasure Pier. The Looff Hippodrome still stands at the beginning of the pier, though the original carousel has been replaced. Photo by Danny Jensen.

To play the Lite-a-Line, you pull on a pinball-like plunger to launch a shiny metal ball up a rounded track, which drops the ball onto an inclined, glass-topped board that resembles a barebones pinball machine. The ball then bounces off a line of rubber bumpers, and (hopefully!) into one of the holes along two horizontal rows, each with a designated color and number. When you sink a ball, the corresponding color and number light up on the five-by-five board (now a computer screen) above the game. The first player to "lite" five numbers in a "line" (horizontally, vertically, or diagonally) wins. Each game costs $1.25 to play, which you pay using a special ID card with your photo, and the winners are awarded the grand prize, a minimum of $15, though the prize can climb higher in progressive games. The game can be frustrating to learn, but once you get the hang of it, it's a blast.

When you take a break from playing, be sure to explore the area surrounding the game tables, where you'll find plenty of memorabilia from the Pike. The displays include historic signs and vintage photographs, carousel horses along with Charles Looff's woodcarving tools and toolbox, a roller-coaster car from the Pike's Cyclone Racer, bumper cars, hand carved heads from a funhouse, and plenty more.

THE LOS ANGELES BREAKFAST CLUB

Where can you have breakfast and learn a secret handshake?

You can tell by the long lines at brunch hotspots and old-school diners that Angelenos love a good breakfast. But there's only one place in LA where you can grab a hot morning meal and also join in a sing-a-long, hear a fascinating talk from a guest speaker, and meet new friends. And while the club's membership has included its share of famous names, just don't expect to spot Molly Ringwald or Emilio Estevez at this Breakfast Club.

Nearly a century old, the Los Angeles Breakfast Club is a wonderfully quirky, under-the-radar gathering that takes place every Wednesday morning in Friendship Hall at the southeast corner of Griffith Park. The nonpolitical, nonsectarian organization began in the early 1920s when prominent businessmen and civic leaders would meet for breakfast after riding the park's trails on horseback, gathering around a chuck wagon run by local banker Marco Hellman. The club was officially founded in 1924, and its meetings soon included music and talks with a roster of early members that included Edward L. Doheny, Cecil B. DeMille, and brothers Jack and Harry Warner. The club grew and prospered, soon building a headquarters (the "Pavilion of Friendship") across from the park's riding academy and welcoming big-name entertainers and notable guests, including president Calvin Coolidge. The meetings were eventually even broadcast on the radio.

The membership ceremony for the Los Angeles Breakfast Club includes sitting on Ham, a wooden hobby horse, while sticking one hand in a plate of eggs.

The foundation of the Los Angeles Breakfast Club has always been friendship, good-natured silliness, and plenty of jokes about ham and eggs. Photo by Danny Jensen.

THE LOS ANGELES BREAKFAST CLUB

What: A long-running gathering for those who enjoy breakfast, quirky traditions, and civic engagement

Where: 3201 Riverside Dr.

Cost: $15 cash

Pro Tip: Check the group's website for upcoming speakers.

During the Great Depression, the Breakfast Club lost its meeting place as membership dwindled. After temporarily relocating to the Ambassador Hotel, the club eventually returned to a location near Griffith Park in 1937 and built its permanent and current headquarters in 1965. While the group had long welcomed women as guests, it wasn't until 1978 that they were able to join as members. And while the club again faced an uncertain future in the early 2000s, the current president, actress Lily Holleman, helped revive the group's momentum, partly by turning to social media to attract new and younger members.

Beginning promptly at 7 a.m., members and guests gather for a breakfast buffet, followed by singing, light calisthenics (don't worry—you probably won't break a sweat), zany traditions, and plenty of merry-making. Without giving too much away, be prepared to recite a cryptogram involving ham and eggs, sing sea chanties, and learn a secret handshake. Guest speakers cover a diverse range of topics, including everything from Hollywood history and LA architecture to robotics and Zen meditation. It's an amazing opportunity to gain a deeper understanding and appreciation for Los Angeles and the world at large while also becoming part of an enthusiastic and welcoming community.

THE WHISKY & POETRY SALON

Where can you enjoy a rare tipple while taking part in a lively poetry reading?

For as long as bards have been reciting verses to all those who care to listen, strong spirits have inspired many to pour their heart into poetry. But these days, it's not often that sipping booze is associated with reading poetry—an activity usually relegated to English classes and quiet cafes. Thankfully for those of us who appreciate both a great glass of whiskey and the well-written word, the Whisky & Poetry Salon brings together two wonderful pastimes in one joyous evening.

Founded in 2012 by writer Kim Ohanneson, the Whisky & Poetry Salon takes place every other month at unique locations around Los Angeles. Past venues have included a historic 1920s loft, Union Station, and the speakeasy-style whiskey haven Bar Jackalope. Guests are invited to bring a poem—original or not—and in exchange for reading the poem aloud to a circle of fellow enthusiasts, they receive a flight of top-shelf and rare whiskey. (And in case you're wondering, most US and Irish producers spell the spirit with an "e" while those in Scotland, Canada, India, and Japan tend to leave it out.) The tastings are often led by brand ambassadors who sometimes

THE WHISKY & POETRY SALON

What: An inspiring evening where guests trade words for whiskey

Where: Locations vary; to find out the next location and register to attend, email Kim Ohanneson at whiskyforwords@gmail.com.

Cost: $35 per person and a poem of your choosing (price may vary for special events)

Pro Tip: Bring a friend and take a ride share so you can soak up the evening and not worry about driving.

bring bottles to taste that might not be available to the public or are hard to find. Light bites are also included in the evening.

Don't be intimidated if you've never read a poem aloud in front of strangers or if public speaking isn't usually your thing. Ohanneson and regular attendees help create a welcoming environment that puts even the most anxious readers at ease. You won't encounter a microphone or bright lights, and there's no need to memorize—plus the tastings help provide a bit of liquid courage. "It's a painless way for people to get to know poetry," explains Ohanneson. "Come for the whisky, stay for the poetry."

The poem you select is completely up to you. It could be something you've written, a childhood favorite, or a recent discovery. And have fun with picking one out; as Ohanneson says, "Finding a poem is an artistic act." The salon offers a chance to sample whiskey you might not otherwise try, hear engaging poems from others, and take part in an inspiring community of like-minded tipplers.

The Whisky & Poetry Salon anniversary celebrations also offer attendees the chance to hear readings from local and visiting poets. "There's such a thriving community of poets in Los Angeles that many people aren't aware of," says Ohanneson.

The Whisky & Poetry Salon is part of Ardent Spirits, an organization run by Kim Ohanneson, which also includes private tastings, curated whiskey experiences, Women Who Whiskey—Los Angeles, and tours of distilleries in Scotland and Ireland.

TOYO MIYATAKE'S CAMERA

Why is there a giant vintage camera standing in a plaza in Little Tokyo?

Little Tokyo is full of countless hidden gems, from secret gardens to out-of-the-way karaoke and jazz bars—not to mention the excellent dining options. But there's one often-overlooked yet significant feature that's hiding in plain sight—*Toyo Miyatake's Camera*. Located in the plaza in front of the Japanese American National Museum, this outsized vintage camera pays tribute to the work of first-generation Japanese American photographer Toyo Miyatake and stands as an important reminder of a dark period in US history.

Born in 1895, Miyatake opened a photography studio in Little Tokyo in 1923 and dedicated his life to documenting the Japanese American community through works of pictorialism, family and wedding portraits, day-to-day activities, and special events such as the Nisei Week parade. However, following the bombing of Pearl Harbor in 1942, Miyatake, along with more than 120,000 people of Japanese descent—two-thirds of whom were American citizens—was incarcerated in one of 10 internment camps in remote areas of the United States.

Miyatake was one of 10,000 people imprisoned at the Manzanar camp in the Owens Valley, where he managed to smuggle in a camera lens and film holder. With the help of a carpenter and mechanic, he constructed a camera out of found scraps. Initially, he took discreet photos of life in the camp and developed the film in secret at night, as what he was doing was illegal. In 1944, Miyatake was able to obtain professional equipment and build a photo studio in the camp thanks to a sympathetic camp director, and he continued to document life inside Manzanar until the camp

Toyo Miyatake was once the official dance photographer for the Hollywood Bowl.

The location of Toyo Miyatake's Camera *is also significant as it was once a reporting site during World War II, where hundreds of Japanese Americans were forced to board buses that took them to internment camps. Photo by Adrienne Florez.*

TOYO MIYATAKE'S CAMERA

What: A replica of a handmade camera used by a Japanese American photographer while imprisoned at the Manzanar internment camp

Where: 369 E. 1st St.

Cost: Free

Pro Tip: Be sure to visit the Japanese American National Museum to learn more about Japanese American history and culture.

closed in November 1945. While there were officially sanctioned photographers such as Dorothea Lange and Ansel Adams who photographed the camps, Miyatake undoubtedly captured a unique perspective from within.

To honor Miyatake's efforts and life's work, the artist Nobuho Nagasawa created a bronze replica three times as large as the camera Miyatake secretly constructed and used in the Manzanar camp. It was dedicated in 1993. Set atop a four-foot-high tripod and made to look like it was made of wood, the camera projects Miyatake's photographs onto a window of what was formerly the Nishi Hongwanji Buddhist Temple, which is now part of the Japanese American National Museum. The camera has a tray of 28 slides that feature photographs not only of the camp but also other events Miyatake documented, including the motorcade of the Crown Prince of Japan in 1931, the 1932 Summer Olympics, and the Nisei Week parade in 1939.

ASTRONAUT ISLANDS

Why can't you visit the resort-like islands off the coast of Long Beach?

Looking out at the water from Ocean Boulevard in Long Beach, you'll notice four islands adorned by palm trees, waterfalls, and soaring white and blue towers that dot San Pedro Bay. What looks like a high-end resort, is in fact, home to around 1,000 fully functioning oil wells.

Nicknamed the "Astronaut Islands," these optical illusions not only help to hide what would otherwise be some unsightly oil production, but they also help keep the city of Long Beach from sinking.

In 1932, the discovery of the Wilmington Oil Reserve, one of the largest in the country, stretching from nearby Palos Verdes through Long Beach, sparked debates over how the community could benefit without covering the landscape in derricks. The region also faced another challenge: it began to sink.

Between 1928 and 1965, scientists observed that parts of Long Beach had sunk by as much as 30 feet due to so much oil being extracted from the subsurface. While offshore drilling in the area was halted in 1956, Long Beach voters approved "controlled exploration and exploitation" in the harbor in 1962, though this time with the use of directional drilling (at an angle) and water injection to replace the extracted oil and prevent further sinking.

To capitalize on the changes, five oil companies formed a company known as THUMS: Texaco (now Chevron), Humble (now ExxonMobil), Union Oil (now Chevron), Mobil (now ExxonMobil), and Shell Oil. The group won a bid to lease the East Wilmington Oil

> ### ASTRONAUT ISLANDS
>
> **What:** Stylish, man-made islands that disguise oil derricks
>
> **Where:** San Pedro Bay, Long Beach
>
> **Cost:** Free
>
> **Pro Tip:** While the islands are closed to the public, you can get a good view of them from Junipero Beach. Be sure to check them out at night, too, when the buildings and waterfalls are illuminated.

Reserve in 1965 and built four artificial islands for extraction. Thanks to a "beautification clause," however, the company had to make the oil operation as quiet and invisible as possible.

Each of the 10-acre islands was designed, with the help of Joseph Linesch who helped design the landscaping of Disneyland, to look like it housed upscale condos with lush vegetation. Condo-like concrete towers mask 175-foot derricks, while curved walls and waterfalls help to muffle the sound. Palms, sandalwood trees, and oleanders, along with 64,000 tons of boulders from Catalina Island, provide additional cover. In 1967, the THUMS islands were each named for fallen NASA astronauts—Grissom, White, Chaffee, and Freemen—and the quartet became known as the Astronaut Islands.

While some longtime Long Beach residents may know the story behind the Astronaut Islands, most people these days are left to wonder what happens on those exotic-looking islands and why they didn't get an invite.

More drilling sites are hidden in plain sight throughout LA, including the Packard Well site in Mid-Wilshire, designed to look like an office building; the Cardiff Tower in the Pico-Robertson neighborhood, made to resemble a synagogue; and the now-defunct Tower of Hope near Beverly Hills High, which features flowers designed by hospitalized children. Many sites are also located in densely populated, often low-income neighborhoods, raising health and environmental concerns and efforts to shut them down.

CROSSROADS OF THE WORLD

What ship-shaped building in Hollywood was the site of a notorious murder?

Countless Angelenos and visitors likely pass the globe-topped tower of Crossroads of the World on Sunset Boulevard without a second thought, but at one time the unique architectural wonder was the hit of Hollywood.

Designed by Robert V. Derrah, who conceived the similarly boat-themed Coca-Cola building in Downtown LA, the complex debuted as a sophisticated shopping center in 1936 centered around a Streamline Moderne building resembling an ocean liner. But prior to construction, a still-unsolved murder took place on the site.

The stretch of Sunset Boulevard was occupied by an ivy-covered bungalow owned by Charlie Crawford, known as the "Gray Wolf of Spring Street" and "Good Time Charlie." In the 1920s, he became the boss of a ruthless crime syndicate known as the "City Hall Gang," and helped run the city from the shadows.

While Crawford supposedly left his crime-filled past with the help of his wife Ella Crawford, he remained entangled in city politics. His reign in LA came to an abrupt end when, on May 20, 1931, he was shot in his bungalow alongside friend and business partner Herbert Spencer. The murders drew national headlines, and the suspected killer, "Handsome" Dave Clark, was ultimately acquitted.

To help move on from the death and drama, widow Ella Crawford hired Derrah to build Crossroads of the World, a stylish shopping center, on the site of the bungalow where her husband was shot.

You'll likely recognize Crossroads of the World from numerous TV and film appearances, including LA Confidential, as well as the music video for "The Globe" by Big Audio Dynamite II.

Crossroads of the World became Los Angeles Historic Cultural Monument #134 in 1974 and was added to the National Register of Historic Places in 1980. (Photo by Adrienne Florez)

CROSSROADS OF THE WORLD

What: A former shopping center shaped like an ocean liner with a colorful past

Where: 6671 Sunset Blvd.

Cost: Free

Pro Tip: Stroll around the property to see the various architectural styles, as well as the 100-year-old valley oak and walnut, avocado, peach, fig, and pepper trees.

The complex centers around the ocean liner-shaped building with red railings and porthole windows, topped by a 60-foot tower with a spinning globe featuring a neon sign that reads "Crossroads of the World." The nine buildings that flank the ship feature an eclectic variety of architectural styles, including Italian, French, and early California styles.

The Crossroads of the World opened in 1936 as a popular destination for celebrities and shoppers looking for a bit of glamor during the Depression. The complex featured artist studios, restaurants, dress shops, a French parfumerie, and a "handkerchief specialist." While the initial glamor faded, the retail shops and studios were eventually converted into offices for the likes of Alfred Hitchcock.

More recently, the offices were used by film and record companies, screenwriters, publicists, and more. The Crossroads of the World has been saved from the wrecking ball several times throughout its existence, and it's expected to be preserved and restored as part of a massive development project that will include apartments, a hotel, and commercial space.

THE GRAPES OF AVILA ADOBE

Why are there grape vines growing above LA's oldest house?

As one of LA's oldest thoroughfares, Olvera Street is a treasure trove of historic buildings, busy restaurants, and colorful stalls. But most visitors don't realize there's a bit of living history growing just above their heads.

Long before Napa and Santa Barbara became renowned for excellent vintages, Downtown LA was the heart of California's wine industry. In the late 1780s, grapes were first planted in Los Angeles by missionaries who brought cuttings from Spain and Portugal. Primarily grown to produce sacramental wine, they became known as "Mission" grapes.

Then in 1831, French-born Jean Louis Vignes (which appropriately translates to "vines"), began growing grapes from his native Bordeaux. He opened the first commercial winery in California in 1833 where Union Station now stands. Vineyards from French, Italian, Mexican, and Anglo growers eventually sprouted up along the LA River. Soon there were more than 100 wineries in LA County, and roughly 75 percent of them were within the city.

THE GRAPES OF AVILA ADOBE

What: A historic grapevine that provides a link to Los Angeles's winemaking past

Where: Olvera Street

Cost: Free

Pro Tip: Be sure to explore Avila Adobe and the many other historic buildings and museums in the area, including La Plaza de Culturas y Artes, the Chinese American Museum, and the Italian American Museum, and grab some taquitos at El Cielito Lindo. If you're thirsty, head to nearby San Antonio Winery or the new Angeleno Wine Company tasting room.

The grapevines above Avila Adobe, which is thought to have been built using tar from the La Brea Tar Pits, clay from the LA River, and wood from the riverbank. An early seal for the City of Los Angeles prominently featured a grape vine. Photo courtesy of Michael Holland.

LA's booming wine industry continued to thrive, but several blights, a demand for land, and ultimately Prohibition led to its downfall. By the end of Prohibition, roughly a half-dozen wineries remained—including San Antonio Winery, which survived by producing sacramental wine and still operates today.

While largely ignored for decades, three ancient grapevines grow above Olvera Street (at one time known as "Wine Street") and behind Avila Adobe, considered the oldest house in LA. The vines are thought to have been planted around the time the house was built in 1818, making them older than the state of California, according to city archivist Mike Holland, who has become the enthusiastic caretaker of the historic vines.

With the help of winemakers, Holland has been cultivating the vines to produce both more grapes and sweeter ones. He's been using the grapes to make small batches of a fortified dessert wine called an angelica, using a recipe from 1891, similar to what the missionaries might have made.

Many streets throughout Los Angeles are named for some of the city's earliest winemakers, including Wilhardt, Kohler, Moss, and, of course, Vignes. Irish-born Andrew A. Boyle was one of the first to plant a vineyard across the river, which is why the area is known as Boyle Heights.

THE MAX FACTOR BUILDING

Where can you see Hollywood memorabilia and learn about the Makeup King?

Much of the glitz and glamour of Hollywood's Golden Era can be attributed to one legendary pioneer of the beauty business: Max Factor. And while you may know his name thanks to the line of cosmetics, you might not know how much he shaped the look of Hollywood icons such as Judy Garland, Bette Davis, and Elizabeth Taylor.

Factor's story and plenty of silver screen memorabilia can be found in the heart of Hollywood at the historic Max Factor Building. Inside the pink and gray building is where Marilyn Monroe became a blonde, Lucille Ball became a redhead, and countless other stars were transformed.

Born Maksymilian Faktorowicz in 1877 in Lodz, Poland (at the time part of the Russian Empire), Max Factor immigrated to the United States in 1904 and eventually settled in Downtown LA. He later moved to Hollywood to provide the burgeoning film industry with his made-to-order wigs and theatrical makeup. Observing that stage makeup, known as grease paint, was too thick and garish for the subtleties of the camera, Factor developed a lighter, easy-to-use version that didn't crack.

In his own cosmetics lab, Factor customized specific formulas and shades for his Hollywood clientele, famously applying the makeup himself to leading ladies Bette Davis and Jean Harlow. As the film industry evolved, so did Factor's products. Eventually, with the help of his son Frank, he developed Pan-Cake makeup for full-color films, a product that's still used today.

Max Factor played an extra in hundreds of silent films, partly because he could easily collect the actors' wigs that he created and bring them back to his shop.

The Max Factor Building was designed by famed theater architect S. Charles Lee in the Hollywood Regency style. (Photo by Adrienne Florez)

THE MAX FACTOR BUILDING

What: A museum of Hollywood memorabilia housed in a historic building of a makeup legend

Where: 1660 N. Highland Ave.

Cost: Adults, $15; students and seniors, $12; children 5 and under, $5

Pro Tip: For more vintage flair with a dollop of kitsch, split a milkshake at Mel's Drive-In in the adjoining building that was once part of the Max Factor facilities.

Pan-Cake makeup turned out to also work well for everyday use, and packaged as a pressed compact was one of the first portable makeup products. Factor marketed the makeup to the public, helping to dramatically popularize daily makeup use with the help of celebrity endorsements. Factor also innovated a variety of other products still used today, including the first-ever lip gloss, waterproof mascara, liquid nail enamel, and camouflage makeup for the marines. Many say that he even invented the term "makeup."

Today, you can learn more about Factor's widespread influence at the Hollywood Museum, housed in the Max Factor Building, and see the rooms where actors and actresses were transformed. You'll also find a "kissing machine" to test lipsticks and a menacing-looking "Beauty Calibrator," designed to measure a woman's face.

The museum also features film props, costumes, and memorabilia from throughout the history of film and television. So even if you're not a makeup enthusiast, there's still plenty to take in, such as Cary Grant's Rolls-Royce, Dorothy's ruby red slippers, and an entire basement floor dedicated to horror films, including the set of Hannibal Lector's jail cell.

HAPPY FOOT/SAD FOOT SIGN

What happened to the sign with a quirky cartoon foot that once told fortunes?

For decades, a huge blue sign advertising a foot clinic stood above the intersection of Benton Way and Sunset Boulevard, slowly rotating to reveal a cartoon foot with a bandaged toe, crutches, and pained expression on one side, and a cheerful, healthy foot sporting gloves and high-tops on the other. Perhaps more than the Hollywood sign itself, this spinning sign, known as the "Happy Foot/ Sad Foot" sign, told the futures of countless Angelenos—until one day when it suddenly disappeared.

Installed in 1986, the sign promoted podiatrist Gary Jamison's Foot Clinic. Jamison enlisted the artistic skills of his son Russell, in elementary school at the time, to design the now-iconic Happy/Sad Foot. While Russell would go on to a successful career in animation, it's one of his earliest designs that would have a lasting impact on LA.

The "Happy Foot/Sad Foot" sign soon developed a cult following as a modern-day oracle. If you saw the "happy" foot, you were going to have good luck that day, but if you saw the "sad" foot, then trouble was . . . afoot.

The sign inspired countless tributes, including costumes, T-shirts, pillows, and even tattoos. The band Eels wrote about the sign in

The Happy Foot/Sad Foot sign inspired a campaign to name the neighborhood "HaFo SaFo." However, the neighborhood, which falls between Echo Park and Silver Lake, really goes by the name Edendale and is regarded as the birthplace of its film industry and gay rights movement, as well as a home to artists, writers, and activists in the first half of the 20th century. Photo by Danny Jensen.

the song "Sad Foot Sign," Beck spoke of its fortune-telling abilities, and it received mentions in novels by Jonathan Lethem and David Foster Wallace. Animator Mike Hollingsworth even created a short animated film of the sign, which became the music video for "Hard World" by LA band YACHT.

While it occasionally stopped spinning (alarming those whose fortunes hung in the balance), it wasn't until 2019 that the sign faced its most foreboding fortune of all: its own demise. Dr. Thomas Lim, the podiatrist who occupied Jamison's former office, was moving. Despite his efforts, he couldn't take the sign with him and new occupants planned to alter it. Hearing that it was under threat, hundreds of fans rallied to save the sign, and artist Bill Wyatt, owner of Y-Que Trading Post in Los Feliz, launched a fundraising pop-up shop featuring items inspired by the sign.

But one day when Wyatt happened to check on the iconic sign, workers were taking it down—coincidentally while Dr. Lim was out of the office. To prevent its removal, Wyatt sat beneath the sign and after several urgent phone calls, took possession of it. Wyatt relocated the sign to his shop on Vermont Avenue, a fittingly quirky gift shop, where it now lives on for all to see. While it no longer spins, it will be preserved for fans to visit and pick up gifts that bear its image.

Anyone who misses the prophetic spin of the Happy Foot/Sad Foot sign's original location can still divine their future at its new home thanks to a smaller version that spins on a turntable.

THE BOYLE HOTEL

Where can you find a community-focused lending library inside a historic hotel?

If you've ever passed through Mariachi Plaza in Boyle Heights, you've likely seen and heard the plaza's namesake musicians, sporting sharp charro suits, and looking to be hired for a wedding, quinceañera, or another celebration. But what you may have overlooked is the Boyle Hotel, a Victorian-era brick building across the street that once housed many of the plaza's mariachi musicians and is now home to a unique lending library.

Completed in 1889, the Boyle Hotel—originally known as the Cummings Block and Hotel—is considered one of the oldest surviving commercial buildings in LA. The Queen Anne and Italianate building was designed by architect William Robert Norton and features beautiful cast iron storefront columns, decorative brickwork, and a distinctive corner turret with a bell-topped belvedere. Positioned atop a hill overlooking Downtown LA, the hotel was built for community leaders George Cummings and his wife Maria del Sacramento Lopez. The building became a social and political hub of the neighborhood, encouraging commercial development of the area.

Beginning in the 1930s, the intersection of Boyle Avenue and First Street became an informal gathering place for mariachi bands to advertise their talents. The Boyle Hotel became a popular and inexpensive place to stay for many of the musicians, earning it the nickname "Mariachi Hotel," and eventually the hotel rooms turned into residences.

In the decades that followed, the building dramatically deteriorated, even losing the top of the corner turret and other

Mariachi Plaza's iconic, hand-carved stone kiosk, designed for musical performances, was donated by the city of Jalisco, Mexico, considered the birthplace of mariachi music.

Head next door to La Monarca Bakery and Cafe for freshly baked pan dulce, horchata lattes, tacos, tortas, and other delicious treats. Photo by Danny Jensen.

THE BOYLE HOTEL

What: A renovated historic hotel with a lending library and bakery

Where: 1781 E. 1st St.

Cost: Free books to borrow, but the pastries will cost you

Pro Tip: Be sure to grab some of La Monarca's incredible house-made flour tortillas to take home.

decorative elements. Fearing potential demolition, the East Los Angeles Community Corporation purchased the building in 2006, and with the help of the LA Conservancy, secured funding for a $24-million-dollar renovation. The project restored the missing architectural features, and the building reopened with 51 units of affordable housing, a community center, and three commercial spaces.

One of those commercial spaces is now occupied by Libros Shmibros, a unique lending library that "puts low- or no-cost books into all hands, native and immigrant, Eastside and West." First opened across the plaza in 2010 by David Kippen and cofounder Colleen Jaurretche, the new location offers plenty of natural light, rolling ladders to reach shelves of books in both English and Spanish, and space to offer community events, a children's reading hour, writing workshops, and more.

LA'S HIDDEN RELIGIOUS WALL

Where is there a hidden wall that surrounds 100 square miles of LA?

While many of the freeways that crisscross LA have historically divided neighborhoods, some of them have come to serve as part of a unifying boundary for one community in particular—though it's mostly unseen by outsiders.

The Los Angeles Community Eruv is an approximately 100-square-mile symbolic wall, bound roughly by the 405, 101, and 10 freeways (as well as a stretch of Western Avenue and other streets) and is composed of around 60 miles of fencing, hillsides, walls, and heavy fishing wire strung across utility poles. While invisible to most Angelenos, this hidden wall encloses a communal zone for many members of LA's Orthodox Jewish community, allowing them to travel more freely and perform otherwise restricted tasks during Shabbat.

The Jewish Sabbath, which lasts from sundown on Friday until nightfall on Saturday, is a time dedicated to prayer and religious study. According to Jewish law, numerous acts associated with "work" are prohibited during this period, such as driving,

LA'S HIDDEN RELIGIOUS WALL

What: A hidden "wall" that enables Orthodox Jews to carry objects during the Sabbath

Where: You can see the wire of the eruv connecting light posts along Western Avenue between the 10 and Santa Monica Boulevard.

Cost: Free

Pro Tip: Learn more about Jewish history and culture in Los Angeles and beyond by visiting the Skirball Cultural Center, the Los Angeles Museum of the Holocaust, and the Museum of Tolerance.

turning on lights, pushing strollers and wheelchairs, and carrying items outside of the home—including food, books, medicine, and small children. An eruv, however, expands the private space to include everything within the symbolic wall, allowing community members to go outside during the Sabbath, attend synagogue, and participate in other activities.

The Los Angeles Community Eruv was completed around 2003 and took roughly seven years to construct, following lengthy discussions with religious experts and the city. The eruv encompasses Beverly Hills, Westwood, West Hollywood, Hancock Park, Pico-Robertson, and parts of Sherman Oaks and Studio City. A team of rabbis inspect the entire perimeter of the eruv weekly— sometimes by helicopter—to ensure that it hasn't been broken. If they find a break, a team of Caltrans-approved contractors are sent out to repair it before the Sabbath. Members of the community can even call a hotline or check the LA Community Eruv website to make sure the eruv is up and unbroken.

So, while the eruv may remain hidden to many in LA, for the thousands of Orthodox Jews in the area who use it, it allows them to remain observant while dealing with the practicalities of daily living.

The Los Angeles Community Eruv is considered the largest eruv in the United States and possibly the world. Other eruvs in Southern California can be found in the San Fernando Valley, Long Beach, and Orange County.

THE WITCH'S HOUSE

How did a fairy-tale home wind up in swanky Beverly Hills?

Just a few blocks from Rodeo Drive, nestled among the upscale homes of brick and white pillars, stands a wonderfully wild house that looks like it was torn from the pages of Grimms' fairy tales or a Disney movie. And, in fact, the fantastical house—with its haphazard-looking shingles on a steeply pitched roof that resembles a witch's hat—was built as a silent film set.

The Witch's House, also known as the Spadena House (more on that later), was originally built in 1920 for Willat Productions on Washington Boulevard in Culver City by the silent film production company's art director, Harry Oliver. The building originally served not only as a film set—possibly making its first appearance in the 1921 film *The Face of the World* and later as the witch's house in *Hansel and Gretel*—but also doubled as offices and dressing rooms.

The storybook-style house (a popular design theme in LA during the 1920s and 1930s) reportedly led to numerous car accidents as drivers gawked at the structure. When Willat Productions shuttered, the building was slated for destruction, but film producer Ward Lascelle bought it, moved it to Beverly Hills, and converted it into a livable home around 1924. During the 1930s, Laschelle and his wife Lillian rented part of the home to a musician named Louis Spadena (also spelled Spadina). In 1938, when the couple divorced, Lillian kept the home and eventually married Spadena, providing the home with another often-used moniker. The couple lived in the house until it was sold to Martin and Doris Green in 1965.

In 1998, real estate agent Michael J. Libow purchased the Witch's House, which he remembers seeing (and being afraid of) as a kid growing up in the area. Rather than tear down the house, as many

---

The original designer of the Witch's House, Harry Oliver, also created the storybook-style Tam O'Shanter restaurant in Atwater Village.

The house has appeared in numerous films, perhaps most recently *Clueless*. It's also considered the most popular non-celebrity house on bus tours. (Photo by Adrienne Florez)

THE WITCH'S HOUSE

What: A wild, storybook-style home from the silent era

Where: 516 Walden Dr., Beverly Hills

Cost: Free

Pro Tip: While the crowds might be too large to get candy, consider passing by on Halloween to see the house in its element.

prospective buyers wanted to do, Libow undertook a massive, five-year renovation of the structure, gutting the uninspiring 1960s remodel and red shag carpets. Inspired by the organic look of Antoni Gaudi's legendary Passeig de Gràcia, which appears to emanate from the ground, Libow enlisted film production designer Nelson Coates and landscape designer Jane Marshall, along with other artisan designers, to revamp the home inside and out. While the home is closed to the public, the interior now features stunning woodwork, colorful tile designs, and curving hobbit-like walls, doorways, and fireplaces with nary a right angle in sight.

Not surprisingly, the Witch's House is hugely popular on Halloween reportedly since the 1930s. Libow has seen somewhere between 3,000 and 5,000 trick-or-treaters stop by for candy during a four-hour period, and he's happy to oblige as the keeper of the Witch's House. And while you can't go inside, there's still plenty to enjoy from afar, including the rickety-looking bridge over a lily-adorned moat, a wooden door with a wrought-iron spider web, a wild assortment of plants, and, of course, the fantastical house itself.

133

THE BATCAVE

Where can you find the most famous cave in Hollywood?

The longer you live in Los Angeles, the more often locations in movies and TV shows look very familiar to you. And one of the most popular filming locations in the city also happens to be one of the least glamorous—a tunnel carved into a quarry wall in Griffith Park known as the Bronson Caves, but perhaps best known as the Batcave.

These famous caves trace their origins to 1903, when the Union Rock Company operated a rock quarry in southwest Griffith Park, an area originally known as Brush Canyon. The excavated crushed rock was used to create embankments and hillside roads for the stylish new housing developments of the Hollywood Hills and to pave Wilshire Boulevard, among other streets. Once it had depleted the best materials, the company abandoned the quarry in the late 1920s, leaving behind a scarred landscape of carved walls resembling an amphitheater and the caves (consisting of one entrance and three exits).

The caves and surrounding amphitheaters soon became hugely popular among Hollywood production companies, serving as a filming location for more than 150 films and TV shows from the 1930s through to the present day. (The earliest film shot there was *Lightning Bryce* in 1919, but filming didn't really pick up until the 1930s.) Filmmakers were drawn to the location for its wild and rugged appearance and mysterious-looking caves that served as the perfect setting for westerns and sci-fi adventures, all within a short drive from the studios.

THE BATCAVE

What: A popular filming location in Griffith Park best known as the Batcave

Where: 3200 Canyon Dr.

Cost: Free

Pro Tip: Look for the concentric circles of rocks on the far end of the caves that look like an alien landing site.

The entrances to the Bronson Caves were typically filmed at an angle so that viewers couldn't see the other end of the cave. (Photo by Adrienne Florez)

The Bronson Caves have made cameos in countless classic films, including *King Kong* (1933), *Invasion of the Body Snatchers* (1956), and *The Searchers* (1956), as well as more recent movies like *Star Trek VI: The Undiscovered Country* (1991), *Army of Darkness* (1991), *Cabin Fever* (2002), and *Hail, Caesar* (2016). The caves have also appeared in dozens of TV shows, including *Bonanza*, *The A-Team*, and *Twin Peaks*. But to most, the location is perhaps most recognizable as the entrance to the Batcave in the 1960s Batman TV series, where Adam West and Burt Ward would emerge from the cave in the Batmobile as Batman and Robin.

To get to the cave and relive a bit of movie and TV magic, park in one of the lots at the end of Canyon Drive and look for a wide, unpaved fire road on the right that curves southeast, just before the beginning of the Brush Canyon Trail that leads to Mount Lee and the Hollywood sign. The gentle, roughly 1/4-mile path will lead you to the large opening of the cave carved into a 100-foot rock wall. At the far end of the 50-foot tunnel, there are three exits. One is large enough to walk through, but for the other two, you'll have to crouch. As an added bonus, when you come out on the other side, you'll catch one of the best views of the Hollywood sign directly ahead.

Actor Charles Bronson supposedly took his stage name from the same boulevard that Bronson Canyon was named for, as it's also the name of one of the gates into Paramount Studios.

THE BUNNY MUSEUM

Where can you find the world's largest collection of bunny memorabilia?

Some people collect coins and stamps, and others hunt for antiques and autographs. But for one couple in Altadena, the obsession is singular: all things bunny. What started as a small romantic gesture has multiplied like, well, rabbits, growing into a massive collection known as the Bunny Museum, where you can tour the bewilderingly large and diverse array of bunny-related items and even pet live rabbits.

In 1993, Steve Lubanski gifted his girlfriend (now his wife) Candace Frazee a stuffed bunny for Valentine's Day, preferring it over the commonplace teddy bears. It was also particularly fitting, as she referred to him as her "honey bunny." The heartfelt gesture set in motion a bunny-themed gift-giving trend, beginning with holidays (first Easter, of course), and eventually leading to a daily exchange of bunny-related gifts between the couple. The couple even received rabbit-themed wedding gifts, along with a carrot cake for the celebration, naturally.

Over the years, the couple's bunny obsession grew to take over their home in Pasadena, and they eventually decided to open the collection to the public, opening a nonprofit museum in 1998. As the collection continued to expand and enthusiasm from visitors grew, the pair decided to move to a larger space in Altadena in 2017. The 7,000-square-foot exhibition space, a former art gallery, contains 16 floor-to-ceiling salon-style galleries, featuring more than 37,754 (and counting) bunny-related items, divided into more than 100 categories. Yes, it's a lot to take in. But it's an impressive tribute

Members of the Bunny Museum can attend special night parties on Valentine's Day, Easter, and Christmas, as well as a Summer Sock Hop.

THE BUNNY MUSEUM

What: The "hoppiest" place in the world

Where: 2605 Lake Ave., Altadena

Cost: Adults/teens (13 and up), $12; Seniors and Military, $10; Children 5–12, $8; Children 4 and under, free

Pro Tip: Be sure to use "The Bunny Bump" as a greeting when you arrive by making bunny ears with your index and middle fingers, followed by a fist bump.

to bunnies and the couples' devotion to one another.

As you wind through the sprawling collection, you'll encounter all manner of bunny-themed items, including figurines, framed artwork, lunch pails, puzzles, cookie jars, music boxes, books, kitchenware, toiletries, and, of course, lots of plush bunnies. Exhibits also feature the myriad ways in which rabbits have been depicted in art, advertising, popular culture, fashion, folklore, superstition, and everyday vernacular. Things take a decidedly darker turn when you enter the Chamber of Hop Horrors, a gallery dedicated to exposing the mistreatment and negative depictions of rabbits, such as lab testing, "lucky" rabbit foot keychains, and horror films. In another gallery, known as "The Warren," you'll find live Flemish Giants, a large domestic breed of rabbits, who are litter-boxed trained.

THE LIZARD PEOPLE BENEATH FORT MOORE

Did an advanced race of people live in gilded underground tunnels beneath LA 5,000 years ago?

Los Angeles is full of urban legends and lore—it is, after all, a city of reinvention and fantasy. But there's one tall tale that's persisted for nearly a century: the underground tunnels of the "lizard people."

The legend goes that a superior race of "lizard people" related to the Mayans created a vast underground city beneath present-day LA—one of several along the Pacific coast—roughly 5,000 years ago. Not to be confused with reptilian aliens of other conspiracy theories, this was a group of intellectually advanced humans who worshiped the lizard as a symbol of longevity and built subterranean cities in the shape of the reptile. The group allegedly fled areas of the Southwest following a disastrous meteor shower and moved underground to shelter against future catastrophes.

The lizard people supposedly used mysterious chemicals to dig an underground labyrinth of roughly 280 tunnels with enormous chambers for 1,000 families to live on stores of food and water—and vast amounts of gold. The "head" of the lizard-shaped network of tunnels was said to be around Elysian Park or Mount Washington, and the tail stretched to

THE LIZARD PEOPLE BENEATH FORT MOORE

What: An urban legend of an underground city and rooms full of gold beneath LA

Where: Fort Moore Pioneer Memorial, 451 N. Hill St.

Cost: Free

Pro Tip: Get a close look at the memorial to the Mormon Battalion and the New York Volunteer American forces that first raised the US flag atop Fort Moore Hill on July 7, 1847. The memorial includes a waterfall feature that had been turned off for 42 year until recently.

"There's gold in dem thar hills!" Are there still tunnels of gold beneath the Fort Moore Pioneer Memorial? Photo by Danny Jensen.

where the Central Library stands today. Around the Second Street tunnel was said to be a "Key Room" full of riches and 37 four-foot-long tablets of gold that told the story of human civilization.

Who do we have to thank for this fantastical yarn? George Warren Shufelt, a mining engineer and geophysicist, who in the 1930s became convinced of the tunnels after talking to Chief Green Leaf, a Hopi tribesman in Arizona—though the chief's existence was never confirmed. Armed with an ancient sheepskin map and his "radio X-ray machine," which he claimed could detect tunnels and gold, Shufelt convinced the city to allow him to dig beneath Fort Moore Hill, agreeing to split the findings. While it's unclear if the county bought the lore, rumors of buried treasure beneath the hill had long persisted, either left by the Spanish or later by American troops during the Mexican-American war. The city was also carving up the hill, once home to grand mansions, to make way for new roads, so a little more digging couldn't hurt.

On March 3, 1933, a 22-foot shaft was sunk into the Fort Moore Hill. And while the week-long dig attracted plenty of onlookers, alas, no gold-filled catacombs were found. Shufelt tried again, this time digging 250 feet below the hill, but boulders and mud prevented him from going further. The treasure hunt was soon abandoned, and while a drawing of the map still exists, and other attempts have allegedly been made, no one has found the city of the lizard people—yet.

The quest for the lizard people's treasure and tunnels became a huge spectacle and source of intrigue for Angelenos at a time when the country was in the grips of the Great Depression.

HOLLYWOOD HERITAGE MUSEUM

Where can you find memorabilia from Hollywood's earliest days in a historic barn?

On your way to the Hollywood Bowl, you may have spotted a small, clapboard building across Highland Avenue. But you may not have realized that the distinguished-looking barn is the oldest existing motion picture production building in Hollywood and now holds treasures of Tinseltown.

Built in 1901 for Col. Robert Northam, the barn originally stood near Vine Street and Selma Avenue, surrounded by a lemon grove. The property was later sold to realtor Jacob Stern who leased the barn to the Burns and Revier Studio, the second movie studio in Hollywood (following the Nestor Film Company). The barn, which contained an office, dressing rooms, and editing rooms, soon became home to the Jesse L. Lasky Feature Play Company. The company used the barn in its first feature, the 1914 film *The Squaw Man*, codirected by Cecil B. DeMille and considered the first feature-length film shot entirely in Hollywood. DeMille apparently grew quite fond of the barn, and he even brought it with him when the company relocated.

In 1916, the Lasky Company merged with Adolph Zukor's Famous Players Film Company which later became the Paramount Pictures Corporation. The barn remained on the Paramount lot until 1926 when the company relocated—along with the barn—to its current

When traveling west from New York, Cecil B. DeMille originally considered Flagstaff, Arizona, as the filming location for *The Squaw Man*, but decided the landscape wasn't the right look, so he and star Dustin Farnum hopped back on the train bound for Hollywood.

This 1930s miniature of Hollywood by cabinetmaker Joe Pellkofer is located at the Hollywood Heritage Preservation Resource Center, which is on Hollywood Boulevard and is occasionally open to the public. Photo by Danny Jensen.

HOLLYWOOD HERITAGE MUSEUM

What: Cinema history inside the oldest movie production building in Hollywood

Where: 2100 N. Highland Ave.

Cost: Adults, $7; Children under 12, free

Pro Tip: When you visit, ask about the Hollywood miniature, an enormous and incredible re-creation of the neighborhood in the 1930s by cabinetmaker Joe Pellkofer. The miniature is located at the Hollywood Heritage Preservation Resource Center on Hollywood Boulevard, which is occasionally open to the public.

location on Melrose Avenue. For decades, the barn served as the studio's gym and occasional film set as part of the Western Street backlot.

In 1979, the fate of the Lasky-DeMille barn was uncertain. Paramount donated the building to the Hollywood Chamber of Commerce, and it was left in a parking lot across from Capitol Records. The barn was soon re-donated to Hollywood Heritage, an organization dedicated to saving iconic Hollywood buildings. It was moved to its current location, and after a three-year renovation, opened in 1985 as a museum featuring artifacts from Hollywood's earliest days.

The Hollywood Heritage Museum lets you step inside Tinseltown history, where you'll find historic posters, photos, props, memorabilia, and even a re-creation of DeMille's office. The museum also holds special events and screenings that are open to the public.

BEVERLY HOT SPRINGS

Where can you take a dip in the only natural hot spring in LA?

Most of us have days where a relaxing soak seems like it would be the best remedy. And while there are natural springs throughout California, most tend to require a pricey resort fee or a trek to a remote area. Thankfully, those who know where to look can enjoy the restorative properties of a hot mineral spring—the only one of its kind in the city—hidden inside an unassuming spa on the northern edge of Koreatown.

Long before it became a destination for weary Angelenos, the natural spring was discovered around the turn of the 20th century by prospectors digging for oil. While not as financially rewarding, the strong stream of roughly 100-degree mineral water ultimately proved useful. In 1910, Richard S. Grant encountered the 2,200-foot well when he bought the land around it, a wheat field at the time. The water was then used by residents in the area until city water mains were installed in 1915.

The water from the well was particularly popular among big drinkers, who found that the sodium bicarbonate and other minerals provided relief the next day. For a time, it was even bottled and sold as "Wonder Water." The water was also thought to be beneficial for a variety of ailments, including "acidity, rheumatism, ulcers in stomach, kidney, bladder, gallstones and similar troubles," though the cure-all claims likely wouldn't stand up to modern-day

BEVERLY HOT SPRINGS

What: LA's only natural hot spring, perfect for a long soak

Where: 308 N. Oxford Ave.

Cost: $35 on weekdays; $40 on weekends and holidays; free admission with any treatments

Pro Tip: Take a moment to enjoy the two-story waterfall in the lobby, great for photo-ops to make your friends jealous. And try going during the week when it's not as busy.

regulations. Business slowed after World War II, however, and the flow of the spring was reduced and largely forgotten.

Decades later, the well was rediscovered when Yang Cha Kim and her husband Chang Bum Huh heard rumors of a natural hot spring soon after opening a restaurant on Olympic Boulevard in the late 1970s. Following a tip about the well's location, Kim, who holds a degree in traditional Korean medicine, and Huh, who was a weightlifter for Korea in the 1964 Olympics, bought the property and built the Beverly Hot Springs spa.

Today, visitors can let their worries and tension melt away in mineral-rich, geothermally heated pools fed by tile-lined fountains and surrounded by faux-rock walls and plants. The naturally occurring sulphur and silica in the mineral water can help refresh and rejuvenate your skin, so you might say the fountain of youth is right here in LA. You can follow up your soak by taking a cold plunge or head to the steam room or sauna. Those looking for more pampering can sign up for vigorous body scrubs, massages, facials, and other treatments.

An analysis in 1931 found that in addition to sodium bicarbonate (the primary mineral), the alkaline spring water contains silica, iron and aluminum oxides, magnesium carbonate, sodium bicarbonate, sodium carbonate, sodium sulfate, and sodium chloride.

143

LOS ANGELES PET MEMORIAL PARK

Where can you pay tribute to some of Hollywood's famous four-legged stars?

Los Angeles is home to many historic and star-studded cemeteries, but there's one final resting place where many Hollywood celebrities of the furrier sort can be found: the Los Angeles Pet Memorial Park in Calabasas.

Founded in 1928 by veterinarian Dr. Eugene Jones, whose clientele included many of early Hollywood's animal stars and the pets of big-name performers, the cemetery was created as a place where pet owners could pay tribute to their little loved ones who might not otherwise have such a dignified resting place. At the time, laws prohibited the burial of animals within city limits, so Jones purchased a 10-acre plot of land in rural Calabasas. Small plots went for as little as $12.50 (about $180 today), while those able to splurge could spring for a $400 spot (about $6,000 today) in the distinguished mausoleum.

The Pet Memorial Park's earliest celebrity residents included Tawny, one of the MGM lions; Jiggs, who played "Cheetah" in *Tarzan*; and Pete the Pup from *Our Gang*. The beloved pets of many of Hollywood's onscreen legends that were interred there include Kabar, Rudolph Valentino's Doberman Pinscher; Boogie,

A striped tabby cat by the name of Room 8 became a local star after he began visiting students at Echo Park's Elysian Heights Elementary School in 1952, returning at the start of every school year and leaving for the summer. Room 8 inspired a book and a documentary, and he was buried at the park in 1968.

The memorial of Tawny, an MGM Lion. Photo courtesy of the Los Angeles Pet Memorial Park.

Mae West's monkey; and Droopy, the champagne cocker spaniel of Humphrey Bogart and Lauren Bacall. The park is also the final resting place for the pets of Charlie Chaplin, Gloria Swanson, and Alfred Hitchcock. Many of the burials were lavish and appropriately dramatic affairs. But in the early 1980s, the fate of the pet cemetery was uncertain.

In 1973, the Jones family donated the Pet Memorial Park to the Los Angeles ASPCA. But a decade later, the organization decided to sell the property. Before developers could snatch up the prime real estate, a group of pet owners formed the nonprofit Saving Our Pets' History in Eternity (SOPHIE) to preserve the park in perpetuity. Some of the park's more recent celebrity burials include pets belonging to Steven Spielberg, Diana Ross, and William Shatner. More than 40,000 pets, both famous and merely famous to their owners, have found their final resting place at the park.

Be sure to take time to see the creative ways owners celebrate their deceased pets with colorful decorations. Yellow flowers are usually a good indicator that the memorial belongs to a famous Hollywood animal.

TANKLAND

Where can you find an impressive collection of military vehicles used both on the battlefield and on the big screen?

Whether you're a military history buff, a veteran or active duty service member, or just have an appreciation for LA's quirkier, under-the-radar exhibitions, the American Military Museum in South El Monte should be on your must-visit list.

Established in 1962 and affectionately nicknamed "Tankland," the outdoor museum features a wide range of more than 180 military vehicles, including trucks, Jeeps, artillery trailers, a motorcycle, a helicopter, boats and amphibious vehicles, and, of course, tanks. You'll also encounter imposing artillery cannons and an extensive bomb collection (thankfully with the explosive materials removed), as well as other military ephemera, including helmets, vehicle parts, equipment, and artillery shells.

The collection includes vehicles and equipment that have been used by the US Army, Navy, Air Force, and Marines, ranging from World War I to Operation Desert Storm. Roughly half of the vehicles are still operational—but don't get any ideas as the beasts of war are off-limits to climbers.

If some of the vehicles look particularly familiar to you, even as a civilian, that's because the American Military Museum frequently rents vehicles, equipment, and props for films and TV shows, photo

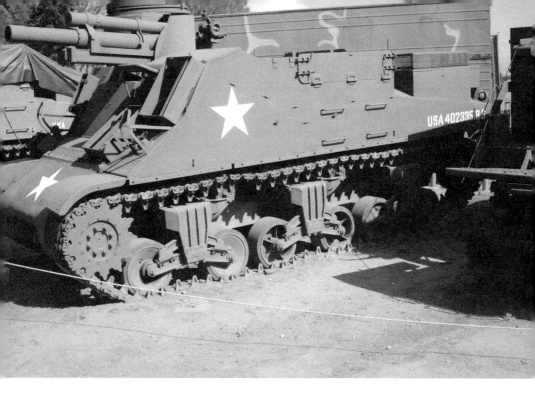

A binder with details on the vehicles and equipment at Tankland is available to visitors for a self-guided tour. And don't forget to check out the small tented gift shop. Photo courtesy of the American Military Museum.

shoots and theater, and wherever else one might need a massive tank. Tankland rentals have been featured in classics such as *Patton* and *M*A*S*H*, as well as more recent productions, including *Fury* and *Straight Outta Compton* (remember the opening scene?). It's a popular destination for school field trips, and the property can also be rented for private events for those looking for an epic military-themed party.

Highlights from Tankland's exhibition include the M47 "Patton" Medium Tank, the M5A1 "Stuart" Light Tank, and the M551 "Sheridan" Light Tank.

LASERIUM

Where can you see a revival of one of the world's first laser light shows?

If you came of age in Los Angeles between November 19, 1973, and 2002, there's a strong possibility that you spent at least one evening gawking at the mesmerizing laser light show at the Griffith Observatory planetarium. And even if you weren't among those wide-eyed (or in many cases, red-eyed) teens who marveled at the swirling and soaring array of colors—often choreographed to classical music as well as the songs of The Beatles, Led Zeppelin, and most famously, Pink Floyd—you'll be happy to learn that Laserium, the live laser concerts that started it all, are back.

Laserium was the futuristic brainchild of experimental filmmaker Ivan Dryer, who in the early 1970s collaborated with Caltech physicist Dr. Elsa Garmire to bring live laser projections to the people. Along with filmmaker Dale Pelton, the group launched Laser Images, Inc., and in 1973, with the help of optical, mechanical, and electrical engineers and artists, debuted "Laserium: The Original Cosmic Concert" at the Griffith Observatory (where Dryer had once worked as a guide). While others had experimented with laser light performances (many of them pre-filmed instead of live) in the years prior, Laserium is considered the first to have commercialized the live laser light show as entertainment for the masses. While it took a bit of convincing to catch the interest of the Observatory, once the show debuted, it was a hit.

The Laserium shows at the Observatory were so successful that they eventually expanded, setting up shows in seven cities across

Laserium inspired countless imitators and led to lasers being used for entertainment as big-name bands incorporated them into shows, including Led Zeppelin, Pink Floyd, and Alice Cooper (who got a hand from Dryer).

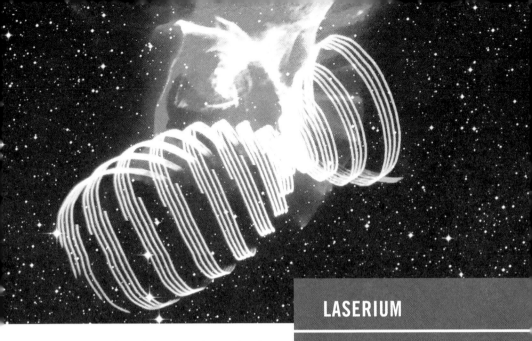

You can almost hear Leonard Nimoy's voice inviting you to "beam aboard" as he once did in the original Laserium ads. Photo courtesy of Laserium.com.

LASERIUM

What: An innovative live laser show that's returned to LA

Where: Find out when and where at Laserium.com

Cost: Check Laserium.com for tickets and pricing

Pro Tip: Follow Laserium on Facebook for performance announcements and to watch some classic clips of past performances.

the country by 1975. Two years later, they were established in 13 venues, including in Canada, the UK, and Japan. But after a nearly three-decade run, with new shows unveiled almost every year, Laserium's residency at the Observatory came to an end in 2002 following a renovation.

But just when it seemed like there might be a future without lasers in Los Angeles, it was announced that the laser beams of Laserium would shine brightly once again. Excitement began to build in 2016, when longtime fans and newcomers were treated to a short-run revival in Van Nuys. And now the Laserium team is hard at work, rebuilding the original Laserium laser projector to be better than ever and making plans to soon relaunch the legendary shows with classic fan favorites and brand-new performances.

THE LOST ZOOS AND ANIMAL FARMS OF LA

What happened to the once wildly popular attractions of lions, and ostriches, and alligators (oh my!)?

These days, the Los Angeles Zoo at the northeast corner of Griffith Park is the city's biggest destination to see wild animals up close. But during the early 20th century, numerous zoos and private animal farms across the city drew enormous crowds.

THE LOST ZOOS AND ANIMAL FARMS OF LA

What: The remnants of LA's old Zoo in Griffith Park

Where: 4801 Griffith Park Dr.

Cost: Free

Pro Tip: Try catching a performance by the Independent Shakespeare Company near the old zoo during the summer.

Before landowner Colonel Griffith J. Griffith donated 3,015 acres of his Rancho Los Feliz estate to the city for a park, the colonel helped establish one of the city's earliest animal attractions: an ostrich farm. In 1885, Griffith partnered with English naturalist Charles Sketchley to create a 680-acre farm on his property. Sketchley imported ostriches from South Africa with the primary goal of selling their feathers, a highly fashionable—and pricey—item at the time for women's hats and boas.

Hundreds of visitors came to gawk at the birds and feed them oranges. Investors even built the Los Angeles Ostrich Farm Railway to ferry visitors to the farm, a route that became Sunset Boulevard. When financial troubles forced the farm to close in 1889, it was not the only game in town. The popular Cawston Ostrich Farm in South Pasadena invited visitors to ride in ostrich-drawn carriages and pose atop a taxidermied ostrich. By 1910, at the height of the craze, there were 10 ostrich farms in LA.

In 1885, Los Angeles also opened the Eastlake Zoo (present-day Lincoln Park). Unfortunately, however, it was considered meager

and cramped. In 1912, the zoo relocated to the former site of the Griffith/Sketchley Ostrich Farm to become the Griffith Park Zoo. The zoo featured bears, zebras, elk, elephants, and even camels, though it continued to be riddled with problems.

Other wild animal attractions included the Barnes Wild Animal Circus and the Selig Zoo across from Lincoln Park, where film producer William Selig showcased more than 700 animals.

From 1907 to 1953, the California Alligator Farm in Lincoln Heights was a hugely popular spectacle, where visitors could watch the alligators perform tricks, slide down chutes, and wrestle with trainers. Guests could also ride on an alligator's back, buy alligator leather products, and even purchase baby alligators. At Gay's Lion Farm in El Monte (1925 to 1942), visitors could see some of the silver screen's most famous cats perform. Meanwhile, at Monkey Island in the Cahuenga Pass (1938 to early 1940s) and the Los Angeles Monkey Farm in Culver City (1929 to the mid-1930s), visitors could toss peanuts to hundreds of primates.

While these attractions are long gone, you can still find evidence of some. In South Pasadena, at the corner of Sycamore and Pasadena Avenues, stands a plaque dedicated to the Cawston Ostrich Farm. And perhaps best known, the eerie remains of the Old LA Zoo can be found in Griffith Park—including bear grottos and cages—left behind when the zoo relocated to its current site in 1966.

You can still find the ferocious-looking concrete lions (created by sixth-generation Italian sculptor Carlo Romanelli) that once guarded the entrance of William Selig's Zoo now standing proud at the new Los Angeles Zoo in Griffith Park.

THE ORIGINAL SPEAKEASIES

Where can you sip hooch in an actual Prohibition-era speakeasy bar?

In recent years, LA has seen a wave of fun and slick speakeasy-inspired bars featuring cleverly disguised covert entrances and elegant cocktails. But finding a bar in LA that served as an actual speakeasy during Prohibition is even trickier than figuring out the secret password to those modern watering holes.

When the Volstead Act went into effect on January 17, 1920, American drinkers were suddenly bereft of places to legally enjoy a tipple. Rather than let that stop them, many Angelenos took the party underground. While many of these speakeasies were lost to time after Prohibition was repealed in 1933, a few have since been uncovered and preserved.

To gain access to some of the city's original speakeasies, check out Cartwheel Art's Underground LA walking tours. These expert-led tours take you through Downtown LA's hidden passageways—service tunnels repurposed to transport booze in secret—to discover long-dormant juice joints. The tour offers an exclusive look at the colorfully adorned basement walls of the King Eddy Saloon, which was converted into a hidden bar during Prohibition while the upstairs saloon became a music store as a front. You'll also get to stand behind the bar of a former speakeasy hidden beneath a hotel—but you'll have to sign up for the tour to find out where.

To get the full speakeasy experience, complete with a glass of hooch, then head to the Del Monte hidden beneath the Townhouse in Venice. In 1915, Italian immigrant Cesar Menotti opened the Townhouse, which quickly became one of the most popular drinking

Rather than putting a stop to drinking in Los Angeles, Prohibition is thought to have doubled the number of drinking establishments in the city as speakeasies sprung up all over.

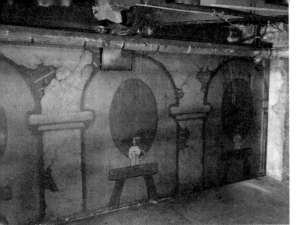

You can still see many of the murals of the former speakeasy beneath the King Eddy Saloon during Cartwheel Art's Underground LA tour, which includes cartoon renditions of Prohibition revelers. And if you look closely, you can even find some vintage graffiti. Photo by Danny Jensen.

THE ORIGINAL SPEAKEASIES

What: Original speakeasies from the Prohibition era that you can still visit

Where: The Del Monte: 52 Windward Ave., Venice; meeting location of Cartwheel Art's tour provided upon booking.

Cost: The price of a drink and the occasional cover charge at the Del Monte; $85 per person for Cartwheel Art's Underground LA Tour

Pro Tip: Check the Del Monte calendar or social media to catch live music, comedy, and more on most nights. To book Cartwheel Art's Underground LA tour check their website: http://www.cartwheelart.com.

establishments in the area and remains one of the oldest operating bars in LA. Rather than let Prohibition slow his thriving business, Menotti quickly converted the upstairs saloon into a grocery and moved his booze operation to the basement. The bar was only accessible by a trapdoor, and guests were lowered down in a dumbwaiter two at a time. Rather than settle for bathtub gin and moonshine of questionable origin (and safety), Menotti sourced his alcohol from ships—often from Canada—that were legally allowed to come within three miles of shore. Small boats would shuttle the spirits underneath the pier, where it was transported through tunnels and eventually to his speakeasy. Fortunately, such covert measures are no longer required to wet your whistle; you simply need to make your way down the stairs (no dumbwaiter required) to the Del Monte. Though it underwent a stylish restoration years ago, the dimly lit bar still maintains an alluringly illicit vibe.

CAMOUFLAGED AIRPORTS

How did Hollywood help to hide some of the world's most historic airports?

If you flew over what is now known as Santa Monica Airport during World War II, you would've been hard pressed to spot anything resembling a runway, much less an airport. That's because, with the help of Hollywood set designers, the airport was cleverly disguised to protect it from a potential attack.

Before becoming one of the grandest optical illusions in LA history, the airport began as an informal landing strip used by pilots flying World War I biplanes, and it was eventually named Clover Field for World War I pilot Lt. Greayer "Grubby" Clover. Then in 1924, aviation pioneer Donald Wills Douglas Sr. made history there when army airmen took off in four single-engine, open-cockpit Douglas World Cruisers, the first aircraft to circumnavigate the globe. Later, Douglas developed the civilian DC (for Douglas Commercial) models, the first of which took off from Santa Monica, forever changing air travel as we know it.

As World War II approached, Douglas's aircraft manufacturing operation rapidly expanded, hiring 44,000 workers to meet wartime demand. But following the attack on Pearl Harbor, Douglas realized his operation was vulnerable to enemy attack. So, Douglas, along with his chief engineer and test pilot, Frank Collbohm; architect H. Roy Kelley; and landscape architect Edward Huntsman-Trout, enlisted set designers from Warner Bros. studios to make the Santa Monica airstrip and facility disappear.

CAMOUFLAGED AIRPORTS

What: Museum of Flying: An aviation museum featuring vintage aircraft

Where: 3100 Airport Ave., Santa Monica

Cost: Adults, $10; Students and Seniors, $8; Children 3–12, $3

Pro Tip: Check the museum's calendar for special events and speakers.

Santa Monica Airport is one of America's busiest single-runway general aviation airports. Photo by Adrienne Florez.

To camouflage the entire operation, the team used millions of square feet of chicken wire, burlap, and camouflage netting stretched across hundreds of tall poles to cover the terminal, hangers, parking lots, and other buildings. The top of the enormous canopy was decorated to look like a hilly neighborhood from above, featuring lightweight wooden houses with garages and clotheslines, faux trees, and phony roads. The runway was even painted green to resemble fields of grass. The disguise was so successful that even their own pilots had a hard time finding the airport.

Douglas wasn't alone in employing such a large-scale optical illusion. Several other aircraft manufacturers across Southern California and beyond used similarly elaborate camouflaging techniques. Some of Hollywood's top set designers helped to disguise other facilities as quaint neighborhoods, including Lockheed in Burbank, North American Aviation in Inglewood, Northrop in Hawthorne, and Consolidated Vultee in Downey.

While the camouflage disappeared after World War II and Douglas Aircraft eventually became Santa Monica Airport (slated to become a public park by 2028), you can learn about the airport's fascinating history at the Museum of Flying, which features vintage aircraft and other artifacts.

Clover Field also made history in 1929 when Amelia Earhart, Pancho Barnes, and other pioneering women aviators took off from the airport for the first Powder Puff Derby, which ended a week later in Cleveland.

THE SPRAWLING WISTARIA VINE

Where can you find the world's largest blossoming plant?

Thanks to our subtropical, Mediterranean-like climate, Angelenos are regularly treated to dazzling arrays of colorful and fragrant trees, plants, and flowers. But there's one vibrant plant that's proven itself to be a particularly hardy resident—the legendary wistaria vine of Sierra Madre.

(While it's commonly spelled wisteria, some botanists and etymologists contend that the plant should be spelled wistaria, as it was named to honor American physician Caspar Wistar [1761–1818], and the altered spelling was an error.)

What began in 1894 as a humble 75-cent vine in a one-gallon container purchased by homeowner Alice Brugman has since grown into the world's largest flowering plant according to the *Guinness Book of World Records*. Wistaria is known for growing quickly— some say as much as 24 inches in a day—and this one certainly did. The vine now covers an entire acre, spanning two backyards with branches that extend more than 500 feet, and at the height of its bloom, the plant has an estimated 1.5 million blossoms. When it was measured by Guinness in 1990, the plant weighed 250 tons, and over the years, it has been nicknamed "Jack's beanstalk," "the monster," and "Lavender Lady," thanks to its stunning purple flowers.

Sierra Madre's wistaria vine is one of the seven horticultural wonders of the world, along with the redwoods of Sequoia National Park, Mexico's Xochimilco floating gardens, Japan's Yokohama rock gardens, Brazil's tropical jungle in the Amazon Valley, India's gardens of the Taj Mahal, and the gardens of Buckingham Palace.

In 1931, the wistaria vine grew so large it destroyed the original home where it was planted, covering the walls and fireplace and causing the roof to collapse. Photo Credit Sierra Madre Chamber of Commerce.

THE SPRAWLING WISTARIA VINE

What: The world's largest blossoming plant

Where: 505 N. Hermosa Ave., Sierra Madre

Cost: Free to view, though shuttle tickets are recommended as parking is limited near the vine

Pro Tip: Check the website of the Sierra Madre Chamber of Commerce for the dates of the festival, and get there early.

Even at a young age, the wistaria was celebrated by the neighboring community. The first occasion was a war fundraiser in 1918 attended by roughly 12,000 people. The festivities grew to a multiple-week celebration and welcomed notable visitors, including Norman Rockwell and Mary Pickford. Vendors sold artwork inspired by the vine as well as wistaria-scented soaps, perfumes, and lotions. In the mid-1940s, it very nearly met its end when a new owner wanted to chop it down, but supporters raised funds to help care for and preserve the vine.

Now one weekend a year—usually in mid- to late March—the current homeowners welcome the public to marvel at the world's largest flowering plant. The event is organized by the Sierra Madre Chamber of Commerce and features food, music, crafts, vintage cars, and more.

THE PINK MOTEL

Where can you find the pinkest vintage motel in LA County?

The world's first motel may have opened further up the coast in San Luis Obispo in 1925, but car-centric Los Angeles has long been closely associated with the convenience and mid-century flair of motor hotels. And while most of the kitschy and iconic motels of LA that sprang up in the post-World War II boom have long been demolished or faded into obscurity, there's one in Sun Valley that still stands as a bright beacon of nostalgia: the Pink Motel.

Originally opened in 1946 by Maximillian and Gladys Thomulka, who moved here from Pennsylvania, the Pink Motel's bold pink and blue exterior and star-topped flashing neon sign easily caught the eye of passing motorists. Situated on San Fernando Road, then known as US Route 99, the vibrant, rose-hued motel was a welcome sight to the many motorists who made their way along the major thoroughfare between Los Angeles and points northward. Starting in 1949, guests could also dine at the adjacent Pink Café, now known as Cadillac Jack's. Beginning in 1959, they could also take a dip in the motel's fish-shaped swimming pool.

While the Pink Motel remained a popular stopover for years, the construction of the 5 Freeway diverted traffic from the area. Many of the surrounding motels and restaurants were demolished over the decades as the area became increasingly industrial, but the Pink Motel managed to survive by catching the eye of Hollywood.

The Thomulkas' son, Monty, took over the property in 1969, and while he continued to rent to guests, he also capitalized on

THE PINK MOTEL

What: A very pink mid-century motel featured in countless film and TV shoots

Where: 9457 San Fernando Rd., Sun Valley

Cost: Free

Pro Tip: While there are no guarantees, if the owners are around—and you ask nicely—they may show you around the property.

The Pink Motel is still a family business, currently owned and operated by Monty's daughter Tonya Thomulka and her son Alex Aprahamian. Photo by Adrienne Florez.

the interest of location scouts in the motel and cafe for production shoots. The motel had made cameos even early on its career, and by the late 70s it became increasingly popular as a location for films, TV shows, commercials, music videos, and photo shoots. From *The Rockford Files* to the recent Netflix series *GLOW*, from *Grease 2* to *Drive*, chances are good that you've seen the Pink Motel and Cadillac Jack's appear on screen a few times over the decades.

And while you can no longer rent a room at the Pink Motel or dine at Cadillac Jack's as they're now strictly used for shoots, it's definitely worth stopping by to admire the stunning colors of this mid-century architectural gem. You're also likely to spot at least a few of the roughly 30 restored classic cars that are available for filming.

After appearing in Stacy Peralta's skateboarding movie *The Search for Animal Chin* in 1987, featuring a young Tony Hawk skating in the fish-shaped pool, the Pink Motel became a legendary destination among skaters and occasionally holds special events.

HOTEL FIGUEROA

Where can you find LA's first hotel built by women for women?

In recent years, Downtown LA has seen a dramatic revitalization with historic buildings given a new lease on life. Among the notable transformations, the stylishly renovated Hotel Figueroa has embraced its progressive roots as a cornerstone for the early women's movement in Los Angeles.

In the early 20th century, the rising number of professional women faced the distinctive challenge of finding safe and comfortable accommodations when they traveled. Most hotels prohibited women from checking into a hotel without a male chaperone, and women were often viewed suspiciously when traveling alone. So in 1925, the Los Angeles YWCA secured $1.24 million to build a 13-story, 409-room hotel to provide a safe haven for women travelers. When the Hotel Figueroa opened in 1926, featuring a lavish Spanish Colonial interior and Italian Renaissance exterior, the *Los Angeles Times* noted it was "the largest project of its kind to be financed, built, owned, and operated by women."

The Hotel Figueroa also featured a writing salon, coffee shop, and beauty parlor, and hosted poetry readings and conferences about sexism, racism, and other social issues. The hotel's manager, Maude Bouldin, was the first woman to manage a hotel in the country; she also flew planes, rode motorcycles, and challenged gender norms that stood as barriers to the advancement of women. The hotel regularly welcomed the California League of Women Voters and other

Look for the original YWCA symbol throughout the Figueroa Hotel: an inverted triangle representing feminine leadership, which can be found over doorways and carved into a fireplace.

HOTEL FIGUEROA

What: A historic hotel built by and for women

Where: 939 S. Figueroa St.

Cost: Free to admire, but room and board will cost you

Pro Tip: Consider making a reservation for Bar Alta, the hotel's hidden 28-seat Art Deco–inspired bar. The bar also features a private room, Casbah, which can also be accessed by a secret sliding bookcase from the Casablanca suite.

progressive organizations, and it was a popular destination for women from around the world.

By 1928, the Hotel Figueroa opened the lower floors to men and their families, but the top nine floors remained exclusively for "business, traveling, and professional" women. But following the stock market crash of 1929, the YWCA lost the hotel, and new owners opened the entire building to men and women. The hotel, however, continued to be a hub for the arts and for political and social organizations until 1958. The Figueroa later became a semipermanent residential hotel and may have been demolished like others nearby were it not for Uno Thimansson, a Swede who became manager in 1976. Thimansson transformed the hotel into a (loosely) Moroccan-themed tourist destination—a design that many people likely remember.

In 2014, the hotel was purchased by Green Oak Real Estate and Urban Lifestyle Hotels, which took on a multiyear renovation to restore it to its original grandeur. The group uncovered the original Spanish Colonial flourishes that had been covered over, while also incorporating plenty of modern touches, including a new two-story pool house/bar by the hotel's distinctive coffin-shaped pool. In addition to multiple stylish restaurants and bars, the redesign also brought back cultural elements centered on women, including art by local women artists and all-women comedy shows.

THE LOTUS FESTIVAL

How did lotus plants wind up in Echo Park Lake?

If you've taken a summertime stroll around Echo Park Lake or cruised around in one of the swan-shaped pedal boats, you may have spotted the spectacular pink and white blooms of the lake's lotus flowers. But you may not know how they got there, how they were nearly lost to time, or the role they play in LA's cultural history.

In fact, the story of how the lotus arrived in the lake is shrouded in a bit of mystery. A 1934 *Los Angeles Times* article points to a 1922 planting, but the exact date remains unclear. The article states that "the rare Egyptian lotus lilies planted twelve years ago in Echo Park Lake are now in bloom." The article continues, "the lilies are tropical plants native to the Nile River Valley in Egypt." Experts, however, have recently identified the lotus of Echo Park as *Nelumbo nucifera*, native to South Asia and Australia and considered sacred to millions around the world, which means they are not the same plant as the Egyptian lotus.

> ## THE LOTUS FESTIVAL
>
> **What:** An annual festival celebrating the blooming lotus plants and Asian and Pacific Island cultures
>
> **Where:** 751 Echo Park Ave.
>
> **Cost:** Admission and entertainment are free, but food and vendor merchandise are not.
>
> **Pro Tip:** Arrive hungry, and be sure to stick around for the performances, dragon boats, and lantern-lighting in the evening.

Whoever planted the lotus beds also seems to be lost to time, though water gardens were fashionable in the 1920s. One legend suggests that missionaries from the nearby Angeles Temple, built by celebrity evangelist Aimee Semple McPherson, brought back lotus seeds from China.

While the blooming lotus flowers were a popular attraction for decades, a celebration for them wasn't official until 1972, when the Department of Recreation and Parks and members of the Council of Oriental Organizations launched the "Day of the Lotus." Renamed

The Lotus flower is significant in many Asian cultures, as it represents rebirth, purity, and life. Photo by Adrienne Florez.

the Lotus Festival in 1990, the annual July event (when the flowers typically bloom) promotes awareness of the contributions of Asian Americans and Pacific Islanders to LA's culture. Each year, the festival is hosted by a different community and features traditional food, live music and dance, arts and craft vendors, dragon boat races, and more.

In 2008, the fate of the lotus flowers looked grim as they had all completely died off, possibly due to pollution or hungry animals. Though the festival continued, many assumed they were gone for good. But when Echo Park Lake underwent a two-year, $45-million restoration in 2011, landscape architect Josh Segal managed to replant the lake with the original lotus plants—thanks to an enterprising thief. It seems, Randy McDonald, a horticulturist from Reseda, had taken a cutting of the plant during the festival in 2005 (not knowing it was illegal) and began growing them to sell at his nursery. McDonald managed to convince the city to buy 371 lotus plants from him—for $30,000— and in doing so, helped bring back the original plant for the rest of us to enjoy for seasons to come.

Originally known as Reservoir No. 4 when it was first created in 1868 as a drinking-water source, Echo Park Lake (and the park itself) was renamed when parks superintendent and landscape architect Joseph Henry Tomlinson supposedly heard his voice echo as he shouted to workers digging the reservoir.

RANCHO LOS ALAMITOS

Where can you walk through thousands of years of Southern California history?

Named for the region's native cottonwood trees, Rancho Los Alamitos in Long Beach offers the chance to get an up-close look at the region's numerous layers of history while touring a working ranch, beautiful gardens, and a historic home.

Rancho Los Alamitos currently sits on 7.5 acres, but the property was once part of the 300,000-acre Los Coyotes land grant awarded to Manuel Nieto in 1790 for the role he played in Gaspar de Portolá's expedition through Alta California on behalf of the Spanish Crown. But long before that, the area was home to the ancestral village of Povuu'ngna, considered to be the traditional place of origin of the native Gabrielino-Tongva people, and it is still regarded as a sacred space by the group.

Over time, Nieto's land grant was reduced and eventually split among his children when he died, creating the 25,500-acre Rancho Los Alamitos, along with four other expansive ranches. Throughout the 19th century, the sprawling ranching and farming property changed hands several times, just as the region transitioned from Spanish to Mexican rule before becoming part of the United States. The ranch's last private owners, the Bixby family, donated the remaining property, which was gradually subdivided and sold over the years, to the city of Long Beach in 1968.

Visitors can now take guided tours through the ranch house, one of the oldest residences in Southern California, which includes the original adobe core dating back to roughly 1804. The Bixby

During the early 20th century, oil discovered under the Bixby's land, including Signal Hill, helped subsidize the creation of Rancho Los Alamitos gardens and other improvements.

Rancho Los Alamitos also offers special tours and school programs that explore the history of the site, including garden walks and a Tongva cultural program. Photo by Danny Jensen.

RANCHO LOS ALAMITOS

What: An educational ranch and garden that showcases many layers of Southern California history

Where: 6400 E. Bixby Hill Rd., Long Beach

Cost: Free (though donations are encouraged)

Pro Tip: You have to pass through a gated community to get to Rancho Los Alamitos; just tell the guard that's where you're heading.

family expanded the ranch house over the years, and it currently includes over 90 percent of the original furniture, artwork, and decor. You can also wander the beautiful four acres of gardens, originally developed by Florence Bixby in the 1920s and 1930s with the help of the legendary Olmsted Brothers. These include a cactus and native garden, rose garden, and, yes, a secret garden. (And don't miss the giant Moreton Bay fig trees behind the home.) Besides the botanical beauty, the property also features restored barns, a blacksmith shop, and corrals, and you'll also meet goats, sheep, ducks, chickens, rabbits, and Preston, the ranch's Shire horse. A Ranch Center also offers special exhibitions, a theater, and a bookshop.

NORTON SALES, INC.

Where can you find props for a mad scientist's laboratory and learn about Southern California's aerospace industry?

Rocket engines, jet packs, satellites, and more—all relics of America's space program—can be found in an unassuming shop in North Hollywood.

Norton Sales on Laurel Canyon Boulevard is the destination for space geeks, star gazers, and anyone looking for authentic-looking props for their next sci-fi flick. It's also the future home of a museum and educational center that will showcase Southern California's rich aerospace history.

First opened in 1963 by Sherman Oaks restaurateur Norton J. Holmstrom, the shop has served as a space junkyard with surplus and used parts from many of the country's biggest space and defense contractors—including Rocketdyne, Douglas Aircraft Co., and Aerojet—which operated in the Los Angeles area. The shop soon became a destination for tinkerers, deep-pocketed collectors, and curious sightseers, both locally and even internationally, in search of deals on space-age parts that originally cost big bucks to produce. Many of the parts come from NASA's legendary spaceflight missions, including Mercury, Gemini, and Apollo.

Norton Sales is now owned by Carlos Guzman, who started as an employee in 1992 and took over the business in 2004, along with his son Roman. Guzman says that over the years, the shop also became a destination for car customizers looking to outfit low-riders with inexpensive, space-age hydraulic valves. The

NORTON SALES, INC.

What: A shop and soon-to-be museum where science and fiction collide

Where: 7429 Laurel Canyon Blvd., North Hollywood

Cost: Free, unless you're tempted to geek out

Pro Tip: Be sure to call ahead to make sure they're open.

shop also became hugely popular with Hollywood's art departments as set decorators and special effects technicians began renting out authentic thrusters, computer consoles, cryogenic equipment, mysterious-looking cases, and all manner of space junk for movies and TV shows you've very likely seen. In more recent years, thanks to a renewed interest in space travel, it's become a treasure trove for engineers from space programs such as SpaceX looking to reverse-engineer early designs.

Now, Guzman is focusing on converting the 3,000-square-foot showroom into the Valley Rocket Center, a museum and learning center. The center will be open to the public, where they can learn about Southern California's aerospace history and get to see and touch rare Apollo-era artifacts. It will also host tours of students from elementary through high school, so that students can learn about the history and be inspired to study engineering, science, and technology. Engineering students and professionals will be invited to join for expert-led and hands-on technical seminars, and collectors will also be able to display or donate artifacts in the museum.

Highlights of the Norton Sales collection include an Apollo command module engine identical to the one that brought Neil Armstrong and Buzz Aldrin back to earth. You'll also find a Rocketdyne J-2, a rocket engine used by NASA's Saturn V launch vehicles and one of the most powerful rockets ever used in the space program.

THE WILLIAM MULHOLLAND MEMORIAL FOUNTAIN

Where is there a fountain dedicated to the controversial figure that brought water to a growing Los Angeles?

Where Los Feliz Boulevard meets Riverside Drive, the soaring spray of a fountain may have caught your eye. Maybe it dazzled at night with red and green lights—earning the nickname "the Kool-Aid fountain." However, more recently, the circular turquoise fountain probably sat still.

Designed by Walter S. Claberg in 1940, the fountain is dedicated to William Mulholland, the "father of the Los Angeles water system," who engineered the 233-mile-long Los Angeles Aqueduct. Mulholland's ambitious, yet problematic project provided the city with the majority of its water supply, enabling LA's rapid population growth.

Cutting through mountains, Mulholland's aqueduct brought water from the Owens River Valley to LA through pipelines and tunnels. At the opening ceremony in 1913, Mulholland famously shouted, "There it is—take it," as the water flowed.

To obtain the water, however, Mulholland used bribery and deception to secure water rights from Owens Valley farmers (who initially stole the land and water from the Paiute Indians). The project

---

In 1976, when the Los Angeles Department of Water and Power planned to draw more water from the Owens Valley, an arrow tied with a stick of dynamite was shot into the Mulholland Fountain by an activist—but it failed to detonate. To this day, residents of the area and environmental groups continue to fight to address the ongoing impact of the aqueduct on the Owens Valley.

It's thought that when Mulholland was a ditch-cleaner for the "zanja madre" he lived in a small shack near his present-day namesake 50,000-gallon fountain. Photo by Danny Jensen.

THE WILLIAM MULHOLLAND MEMORIAL FOUNTAIN

What: A fountain dedicated to the "father of the Los Angeles water system"

Where: Riverside Drive at Los Feliz Boulevard

Cost: Free

Pro Tip: You can take a self-guided audio tour of the entire aqueduct to learn about its history and impact by visiting thereitistakeit.org.

diverted water from the area, turning Owens Lake into dusty salt flats, and inciting California's "Little Civil War" as residents fought back. When lawsuits didn't work, activists dynamited the aqueduct. These water wars inspired numerous books and movies, most famously *Chinatown*.

When Mulholland died in 1935, however, much of the controversy was washed over. In 1940, thousands gathered for the dedication of the William Mulholland Memorial Fountain.

The fountain became a popular destination during hot summers, but in recent decades, the memorial deteriorated. Following a renovation in 2013, the fountain reopened with a new drought-tolerant Aqueduct Centennial Garden. The garden features a 233-foot concrete curb embedded with blue glass, echoing the length and path of the aqueduct. Nearby stands a section of the original aqueduct pipe, and a circular slab embedded with Mulholland's words, "There it is—take it."

169

GREYSTONE MANSION

Where can you tour the gardens of a palatial home where a mysterious murder took place?

Despite sprawling acreage and a tale of murder, the massive Doheny Mansion is often overlooked amongst its relatively diminutive neighbors in Beverly Hills. The storied estate, however, is in fact a beautiful public park with meditative gardens, sweeping city views, and Hollywood history.

Finished in 1928, the 46,000-square-foot Greystone Mansion was a gift to Edward "Ned" Laurence Doheny, Jr. from his father, legendary oil tycoon Edward Laurence Doheny. Doheny Sr. and friend Charles A. Canfield were the first to strike oil in Los Angeles, and later in Mexico, becoming the largest oil producers at the time.

The 55-room Tudor Revival-style mansion, the centerpiece of the 429-acre Doheny Ranch, was designed by Gordon B. Kaufmann (known for the Hoover Dam and *Los Angeles Times* building). The home's name was inspired by the grey Indiana limestone which covers its three-foot-thick concrete walls. The interior features hand-carved oak, marble floors, secret passageways, an underground bowling alley with a Prohibition-era bar, and a movie theater. The immaculate grounds, designed by Paul G. Thiene, originally included terraced gardens, elegant fountains, a swimming pool, riding trails, and an 80-foot waterfall (sadly no longer there).

On the night of February 16, 1929, five months after Ned and his wife Lucy moved into the mansion with their five children, Ned was found shot to death, along with his secretary and confidant Hugh

---

Greystone Mansion's bowling alley was famously used for the final scene of *There Will Be Blood*, which was based on Upton Sinclair's *Oil!*, a novel that many believe was inspired by Edward Laurence Doheny.

Exploring the spectacular grounds of Greystone Mansion offers a quiet escape in the midst of the city, while also offering a glimpse of the grandeur and opulence of a bygone era.

GREYSTONE MANSION

What: A historic and storied mansion with beautiful gardens.

Where: 905 Loma Vista Dr, Beverly Hills

Cost: Free; advance reservations required

Pro Tip: While the grounds of Greystone are open to the public, the mansion interior is only open occasionally for tours and special events, so keep an eye out for opportunities to go inside.

Plunket. While the official story stated that an allegedly unhinged Plunket shot Doheny before killing himself, many have questioned the unusual circumstances and inconsistencies in the crime scene findings.

Following the deaths, Lucy lived at Greystone with her children until 1955 when she and her second husband, Leigh Battson, sold the vast majority of the Doheny Ranch. The City of Beverly Hills eventually purchased the remaining 18.3 acres and the mansion in 1965. The city then leased it to the American Film Institute as a campus from 1969 to 1982, when it served as a training ground for some of Hollywood's biggest names.

In 1971, the site was dedicated as a public park and in 1976 Greystone was added to the National Register of Historic Places. The mansion and grounds have been featured in numerous movies, from *The Witches of Eastwick* to *The Big Lebowski*, and TV shows, including *Alias* and *Gilmore Girls*.

SECRET GARDENS

Where can you find gardens hidden around LA for quiet refuge?

For a city often criticized for its freeways and traffic, Los Angeles is thankfully blessed with green spaces that offer much-needed respite. And while numerous botanical gardens, including The Huntington, Descanso Gardens, and the LA County Arboretum, offer a welcome escape, its LA's more hidden and lesser-known gardens that offer a more secluded—and often free—visit.

Rather than focus on just one secret garden, here are a few options of many around town:

Blue Ribbon Garden (Walt Disney Concert Hall, Downtown LA)

Wrapped around the iconic Frank Gehry–designed venue, this nearly one-acre gem features lush landscaping with flowering trees. Don't miss the giant rose-shaped fountain, a tribute to Walt Disney's late wife Lillian, featuring a mosaic of Royal Delft porcelain vases and tiles. Free and open to the public, except during and 90 minutes before performances.

Garden of Oz (3040 Ledgewood Dr., Hollywood)

Created by Gail Cottman, this whimsical garden hidden in Hollywoodland features an appropriately yellow-tiled path that winds around concrete garden beds, walls, stairs, and thrones adorned by mosaics made of thousands of colorful tiles, toys, and more. Besides paying tribute to the "Wizard of Oz," the garden also features thrones to Rosa Parks, Elvis Presley, the Dalai Lama, and others. Free, but only open on Thursdays from 10 a.m. to noon.

James Irvine Japanese Garden (Little Tokyo)

Inspired by the gardens of Kyoto, this sunken garden is tucked away below street level at the Japanese American Cultural and Community Center. Also known as Seiryu-en or "Garden of the Clear Stream," this tranquil hideaway features a 170-foot cascading stream with a

A peaceful escape in Little Tokyo. © JACCC James Irvine Garden (Seiryu-En) Garden of the Clear Stream Designed by Dr. Takeo Uesugi.

SECRET GARDENS

What: Verdant oases hidden throughout LA

Where: Multiple locations

Cost: Free

Pro Tip: Be sure to check before visiting that the gardens are open and accessible.

babbling waterfall, cedar bridges, stone lanterns, and intricately landscaped greenery. Free and open to the public Tuesday through Sunday from 10 a.m. to 4 p.m., except during private events.

Other excellent secret gardens worth exploring include Amir's Garden in Griffith Park, the Mildred E. Mathias Botanical Garden on the UCLA campus, the Arlington Garden in Pasadena, the Peace Awareness Labyrinth and Gardens in West Adams, the Self-Realization Fellowship Lake Shrine in Pacific Palisades, and the Museum of Jurassic Technology's Rooftop Garden in Culver City.

THE BISON OF CATALINA

How did a herd of free-ranging bison wind up on Catalina Island?

Just "26 miles across the sea" and an hour-long boat ride away, Catalina Island feels worlds away from LA. And while the stunning Art Deco Catalina Casino, tiki drinks at Luau Larry's, and the island's ziplines can certainly transport you, there's one sight that's sure to take you to another time and place—the island's giant herd of American bison.

Catalina's herd of roughly 150 bison had a bit of Hollywood help to land their starring role on the island. In 1926, 14 of the massive, shaggy mammals were imported from the Great Plains for the silent western *The Vanishing American*. Yet, for such a huge undertaking, the footage of the bison ended up on the cutting room floor. To add insult to injury, the roughly 1,000-pound animals were left behind when filming finished. While more inclined to munch on tall grass, the bison nonetheless managed to flourish, eating the island's coastal scrub.

In the years that followed, the herd grew to an estimated record of more than 500 animals. Unfortunately, the hungry bison took a toll on the ecosystem of the island as they grazed on native plants, compacted soil, and outcompeted other animals on an island known for its rich biodiversity.

In 1972, the Catalina Island Conservancy took over management of the bison, and in 1975, the descendants of chewing gum

---

While on the island, be sure to order a glass of Buffalo Milk, which isn't what it sounds like. Catalina Island's signature drink is a blend of Kahlua, creme de cacao and banana, vodka, and half & half, and is thought to have been invented at the Harbor Reef Restaurant in Two Harbors.

The American bison was declared the country's first national mammal in 2016. Photo courtesy of the Catalina Island Conservancy.

THE BISON OF CATALINA

What: A huge herd of American bison roaming the island

Where: All over the island. Catalina can be reached by boat from San Pedro, Long Beach, Dana Point, or Newport Beach, or by helicopter or plane if you're feeling fancy.

Cost: Hiking permits are free; biking requires $35/year membership to the Catalina Island Conservancy; guided tour costs vary.

Pro Tip: For more wildlife encounters, be sure to explore the other nearby Channel Islands for hiking, snorkeling, and kayaking.

magnate William Wrigley Jr. (who bought the island in 1919), donated nearly 90 percent of Catalina to the conservancy. To maintain a healthy population, the conservancy consulted researchers and determined that 150 animals would reduce the impact on the island. In the early 2000s, hundreds of bison were sent to the Rosebud Lakota Sioux in South Dakota, part of the bison's native range. Eventually, however, the effort proved too costly and stressful for the animals, and a contraception program was started to stabilize the herd population.

Today, visitors can spot the bison herd roaming throughout the island. To see them, you can hike or bike around (with a permit) or take a guided tour in a vehicle. Be sure to bring a camera and stay at least 125 feet away from the bison. They may appear docile, but can get defensive if they feel threatened—and you don't want a 1,000+ pound animal running toward you at 35 mph.

THE WAYFARERS CHAPEL

Where can you find a spectacular wood-and-glass chapel overlooking the sea?

Perched atop a Rancho Palos Verdes bluff, the Wayfarers Chapel offers a unique place of respite for travelers in need of physical and spiritual rest—or anyone in search of a stunning architectural gem, fresh air, and a view. Surrounded by redwoods and overlooking the Pacific, the beautiful, one-of-a-kind chapel features enormous panes of glass framed by soaring woodwork and is definitely worth a visit.

Also known as "The Glass Church," the Wayfarers Chapel traces its origin to the vision of Elizabeth Schellenberg, a member of the Swedenborgian Church who lived on the Palos Verdes in the late 1920s. Schellenberg envisioned a small chapel where travelers, or wayfarers, of all faiths could stop to rest, meditate, or pray. Fellow church member Narcissa Cox Vanderlip, who along with her husband Frank helped develop other landmarks around Palos Verdes, took to Schellenberg's vision and agreed to donate the land for the chapel.

While the Depression and World War II delayed plans for the chapel, the two women, along with other members of the Swedenborgian church, were ultimately able to enlist the talents of architect Lloyd Wright, son of the pioneering Frank Lloyd Wright, for the project. Wright had recently visited a redwood grove in Northern California and was inspired to incorporate the "cathedral-like

THE WAYFARERS CHAPEL

What: A beautiful Lloyd Wright–designed chapel of glass and redwood

Where: 5755 Palos Verdes Dr. S., Rancho Palos Verdes

Cost: Free, though donations are encouraged. The chapel is closed to the public during private ceremonies.

Pro Tip: If you plan to get married at the chapel, reservations must be made 18 months in advance.

majesty" of the enormous trees into his design of the chapel. Wright also looked to incorporate the philosophy of Emanuel Swedenborg (1688–1772), the scientist, engineer, philosopher, mystic, and theologian, who emphasized the harmony of God, nature, and the mind and spirit.

Unveiled in 1951, the completed chapel features a towering framework of redwood with large panes of 1/4-inch plate glass, supported by a foundation of Palos Verdes stone. Wright also had redwood saplings planted around the structure, which have since grown to create a towering canopy above the chapel and can be easily enjoyed by visitors through the glass walls. The chapel is considered to be one of the most impressive examples of Organic Modern architecture, and is listed on the National Register of Historic Places.

The chapel's 3.5-acre site now also features a rose garden, a memorial fountain, a visitor center, a bell tower, and a colonnade, perfect for enjoying views of the ocean.

The chapel is enormously popular for weddings, hosting roughly 800 per year. Famous weddings of the past included Jane Mansfield, Brian Wilson of the Beach Boys, and Dennis Hopper.

HIDDEN STAIRCASES

Why are there so many stairways hidden around LA?

LA is often maligned as a car-centric city—there's even a Missing Person's song that suggests nobody walks here. But the reality is that before traffic and freeways began to congest the landscape, Los Angeles was a city of walkers and public transit takers. Thankfully, it still is for many of us, but many of the trolleys, streetcars, and light-rail systems that once helped Angelenos zigzag across town are now long gone. The good news is that we've been left with hundreds of staircases all over the city and county, relics of another time that are prime spots for exploring, exercising, and, in some cases, public art.

Hundreds of these hidden staircases are scattered throughout Los Angeles, yet most are overlooked by the untrained eye. Many of the stairways were built in the early 20th century, particularly during the 1920s when LA had the largest trolley system in the world, thanks to the iconic Red and Yellow Cars. The stairs offered Angelenos convenient and direct passageways in hilly neighborhoods from their homes to the transit lines, shopping areas, and workplaces. While many of the stairs are concentrated around the steep hills of Echo Park, Silver Lake, and Los Feliz, they can be found all over, from Pasadena to the Pacific Palisades.

Here are just a couple hidden staircases to get you started (and don't forget to bring water and wear comfortable shoes):

The Music Box Steps (Silver Lake)

This iconic set of stairs is named after the Academy Award-winning 1932 Laurel and Hardy short film in which the duo struggle to move a piano up these same steps. Part of a longer loop with multiple sets of colorfully painted steps, the screen-famous stretch is just 133 steps and connects North Vendome Street and Descanso Drive.

Baxter Stairs (Echo Park)

Beginning on Baxter Street near Elysian Heights Elementary, this daunting staircase is not for the faint of heart. This steep set of 231

The elegant Laveta Terrace Stairway hidden in Echo Park. Photo by Danny Jensen.

What: Staircases offering history, views, and a workout

Where: Multiple locations

Cost: Free

Pro Tip: Check out local author Charles Fleming's *Secret Stairs* and *Secret Walks* books, and the SoCal Stair Climbers for maps and group walks of the stairs.

steps climbs up to Park Drive, and while the route is not the most idyllic, you'll be rewarded with spectacular views of Elysian Park and Downtown LA.

While San Francisco gets all the credit for its steep streets, LA actually has several of the steepest streets in the country, including Eldred Street in Mount Washington, 28th Street in San Pedro, and Baxter Street in Echo Park/ Silver Lake.

THE BRUCE LEE STATUE

Why is there a statue of Bruce Lee in the middle of Chinatown?

Strolling the pedestrian walkways of Chinatown's Central Plaza, there's plenty to catch your eye, from strings of bright red lanterns to towering pagoda-style buildings and archways painted red, green, yellow, and blue (illuminated in neon at night). But there's one sight that often surprises many visitors and locals as they round the bend at Sun May Way and Jung Jing Road—a seven-foot-tall bronze statue of martial arts legend Bruce Lee.

The statue was unveiled in 2013, although it wasn't permanently installed until 2018, but its placement isn't the only surprising thing about it. Designed by an artist in Guangzhou, China, the Chinatown landmark is the first statue of Lee in the United States—despite the fact that he was born in San Francisco and is buried in Seattle. But the statue is certainly at home here as Lee also spent time living in Los Angeles, including during his time playing Kato in *The Green Hornet* TV show. And just a few blocks from where the statue now stands, Lee opened a martial arts studio where he taught Jeet Kune Do, the fighting style and philosophy he developed, while also working out at the Alpine Recreation Center. The statue was first unveiled 40 years after Lee's tragic death at age 32, just one month before his iconic film *Enter the Dragon* was set to premiere at Grauman's Chinese Theatre in Hollywood.

A hero and an inspiration to countless people, both for his work on-screen and off, it's no surprise that Bruce Lee's statue is

> ### THE BRUCE LEE STATUE
>
> **What:** A statue dedicated to the martial arts legend
>
> **Where:** 943 Sun May Way
>
> **Cost:** Free
>
> **Pro Tip:** To learn about the history of Chinatown and more, visit the Chinese American Museum at 425 N. Los Angeles St.

The statue of Bruce Lee is more than seven feet tall and weighs an estimated 1,595 pounds. Photo by Danny Jensen.

a popular destination for fans young and old—once they find it, that is. On any given day, at nearly any time of day, you're likely to spot someone posing for a photo there, doing their best to re-create the statue's readied stance and focused gaze.

Any fans looking to actually learn Lee's Jeet Kune Do fighting style can head to the original studio space where he once taught at 629 North College St. More than five decades after it was closed, the studio was reopened by Eric Carr, a student of Jerry Poteet, one of five elite students trained by Lee at the studio and his home.

Poised with nunchaku under one arm and the other with palm facing out, Lee's face looks focused, his muscles are taught, and his pants seem to ripple with movement—betraying the heavy bronze medium. The loose yet ready pose of the statue seems fitting for a fighter who saw strength in the fluidity of water.

THE RUINS OF THE MOUNT LOWE RAILWAY

Why are there abandoned railroad tracks and a foundation at the top of Echo Mountain?

Today, the journey to the top of Echo Mountain in the San Gabriel Mountains requires a rigorous hike. And while the spectacular views are rewarding, there was once a less strenuous—though more elaborate—way up that included trolleys, trams, and a lavish resort. And while the railways and resort are long gone; intrepid hikers can still see their remnants.

In the late 19th century, many Angelenos sought an escape from the industrialized and crowded city. To help them get there, the ambitious Professor Thaddeus S. C. Lowe set out to create a "Railway to the Clouds."

Following successful business ventures on the East Coast, Lowe relocated to Southern California with his wife Leontine in 1888. Lowe soon partnered with engineer David J. Macpherson to develop a mountain railway above Pasadena.

On July 4, 1893, the Mount Lowe Railway opened, affording Angelenos the chance to ascend thousands of feet up into the mountains. Sightseers would first ride an open-air trolley up 2,000 feet through Rubio Canyon. There they would board open funicular cars and travel 3,000 feet further up the steep, 62 percent grade to the top of Echo Mountain.

Visitors would arrive at the Echo Mountain House, a grand 70-room Victorian-style hotel painted a brilliant white, complete

Not one to shy away from heights, Lowe was known for record-breaking hot-air balloon flights and for using the lofty transport during the Civil War, enabling the Union to spy on the Confederacy.

The remains of a rail car that transported visitors up the mountain. Photo by Kristoffer Miller.

THE RUINS OF THE MOUNT LOWE RAILWAY

What: The remains of a once grand mountain-top hotel and railway

Where: The Echo Mountain Trail can be found at the Cobb Estate, at the corner of Lake Avenue and East Loma Alta Drive in Altadena.

Cost: Free

Pro Tip: Be sure to try out the echo phone at the top.

with bowling alley and barbershop. The summit also featured a dancehall, an observatory, and even a zoo. Brave guests could take an electric railcar further up to the Alpine Tavern on Mount Lowe, enduring hair-raising curves and bridges.

The railway and hotel remained popular through the 1920s with roughly 100,000 visitors per year. Unfortunately, a series of fires, floods, and destructive winds took their toll, and by 1940, the Mount Lowe Railway and the hotel were abandoned. The land was donated to the US Forest Service, the remaining buildings were dynamited in 1959.

Hikers can now journey up to Echo Mountain for those same stunning views and marvel at the remains of Lowe's grand plan. There, you'll find abandoned railroad tracks, cable-winding machinery, and the foundation of the hotel.

183

THE OVIATT BUILDING

Where can you swing dance in a historic haberdashery?

Half a block south of Pershing Square, the Oviatt Building stands as a stylish reminder of both a bygone era and an influential figure in LA's high society during the early 20th century.

Once headquarters of Alexander and Oviatt, considered the most prestigious and pricey haberdasheries in LA, the Oviatt building was where the city's wealthiest were outfitted. While James Oviatt, who cofounded the company with Frank Alexander, came from humble beginnings, his building was far from modest.

During a trip to Europe in search of the latest fashions, Oviatt was inspired by the innovative Art Deco designs at the 1925 Paris Exposition. While construction of his Italian Romanesque–styled haberdashery was underway, Oviatt redirected the plans to incorporate Deco designs. To complete his vision, he commissioned French artists, including renowned art glass designer René Lalique.

The Oviatt building featured more than 30 tons of custom-designed Lalique glass, shipped to LA from Paris, including lamps, display cases, and a lavish ceiling for the lobby forecourt. Lalique also designed the building's elevator doors and mailboxes using a new silvery metal known as maillechort. The building also incorporated French marble and English oak featuring carved angels.

The mezzanine and the first two floors of the haberdashery were stunning, but the penthouse, where Oviatt lived, featured even more luxurious detailing. Referred to as a "Castle in the Air," Oviatt's 10-room penthouse featured mahogany furniture, geometric

parquet floors, and Lalique glass throughout. The outdoor space included a swimming "basin," tennis court, putting green, and a "beach" with imported French sand.

Oviatt was known for hosting indulgent parties on his rooftop, where the city's elite would rub elbows with movie stars. Among the many well-heeled clients Oviatt outfitted were many of Hollywood's leading men, including Errol Flynn and Clark Gable. He also reportedly counted Winston Churchill and US presidents among his clients.

The Oviatt Building continued to be a destination for the city's fashionable until tastes changed. Oviatt himself also came under fire for alleged racist and anti-Semitic sentiments, which he denied. After the store closed in 1969, the building began to deteriorate, and much of the famed glass was sold or lost.

Thankfully, the building has been restored several times in recent decades, and many of the flourishes preserved. Those looking to experience the glamour and decadence of the Oviatt Building's heyday can attend the Cicada Restaurant and Club for dinner and swing dancing with live music.

The Oviatt Building has served as the filming location for numerous films and TV shows, including the exterior (and inspiration for the interior) of the Hotel Cortez in *American Horror Story*, *The Artist*, and Julia Roberts's escargot scene in *Pretty Woman*.

THE MISSING CANALS OF VENICE

What happened to the original Venice Canals?

The Venice Canals have long been an iconic LA destination. But the waterways we see today were actually built after the area's original, far bigger canals.

Abbot Kinney, the trendy boulevard's namesake, arrived in Southern California by chance in 1880. After a three-year "vacation" traveling across Europe in his late 20s, the wealthy tobacco tycoon's plans to return east by train were halted by a snowstorm.

While waiting for the weather to clear, Kinney visited a health resort in Sierra Madre—where his insomnia and asthma seemed to be cured by the climate. He promptly relocated to the area, buying a 550-acre property, which he named "Kinneola," and planting thousands of citrus trees and grape vines.

After developing properties around LA, Kinney built a second home in Santa Monica and with his business partner Francis Ryan, developed a beach resort just south of Santa Monica. After Ryan's death, Kinney found himself with less desirable partners. Upon winning a coin toss to divide their property, Kinney chose the marshy, undeveloped southern half. Initially ridiculed as "Kinney's Folly," the savvy businessman soon proved his critics wrong with a new development.

Little evidence remains of Venice's original canals, and most of the original names were changed, except for the Grand Canal, which became Grand Avenue. The circular lagoon became a traffic circle where Main Street, Windward Avenue, and Grand Boulevard meet.

As you stroll the "newer" Venice canals, try to imagine the much grander waterways that came before them. Photo by Danny Jensen.

THE MISSING CANALS OF VENICE

What: The original Venice canals that were paved over

Where: Venice

Cost: Free

Pro Tip: Check out the Venice Historical Society for tours and special events.

Venice of America, inspired by Kinney's time in Europe, opened on Independence Day 1905 and was an instant success. It featured a pier with amusements, a grand auditorium, Venetian-inspired buildings, and, of course, numerous canals dredged from the marshland. The largest, aptly named the Grand Canal, was 70 feet wide and half a mile long, ending in a large, circular lagoon. Visitors could not only stroll along the seven canals and over bridges, but they could also cruise the waterways with gondoliers to guide them.

Soon after, competing developers dredged six adjacent canals, known as the Short Line Canals, that connected with Kinney's waterways to the south. By 1910, the promoters were selling lots of this new "Venice Canal Subdivision."

The new canals hardly hindered Kinney's growing success, but by the 1920s, his canals were seen as an obstacle to the burgeoning era of automobiles and were doomed to become roads. Residents resisted, but ultimately the courts ruled in the city's favor. On July 1, 1929, dump trucks began filling in the waterways, and soon the original canals were gone. The six Short Line Canals, however, were spared, likely because they were still underdeveloped, leaving us to imagine what Kinney's more extensive canals might have been like.

SOURCES

The *Triforium*
https://triforium.la/; https://totally-la.com/the-triforium-sculpture-in-fletcher-bowron-square/; https://www.laweekly.com/look-inside-the-depths-of-dtlas-weirdest-sculpture/; https://www.atlasobscura.com/places/triforium-los-angeles; https://www.kcet.org/shows/artbound/the-triforium-a-second-life-for-los-angeles-polyphonoptic-sculpture; https://triforiumcarillon.com/.

Angeles Crest Creamery
https://www.angelescrestcreamery.com/; https://www.facebook.com/AngelesCrestCreamery/; https://www.latimes.com/food/dailydish/la-fo-co-angeles-crest-creamery-goat-farm-20180811-htmlstory.html; https://www.desertsun.com/story/desert-magazine/2017/03/29/road-trip-regenerative-goat-ranch-angeles-crest-creamery/99799084/; https://www.laweekly.com/restaurants/grazing-with-the-goats-at-angeles-crest-creamery-10110140; https://www.eventbrite.com/o/angeles-crest-creamery-11098711927.

Chicken Boy
https://www.chickenboy.com/; http://www.chickenboyshop.com/; https://www.roadsideamerica.com/story/16764; https://www.kcet.org/youth-voices/interview-with-amy-inouye-future-studio-design-and-gallery; https://www.vice.com/en_uk/article/yvedyw/one-womans-fight-to-save-a-22-foot-tall-fiberglass-chicken; https://www.latimes.com/opinion/la-xpm-2011-mar-14-la-oe-rodriguez-chickenboy-20110314-story.html.

The Mystic Museum
https://beardedladysmysticmuseum.square.site/; https://www.facebook.com/themysticmuseum/; https://roadtrippers.com/magazine/bearded-ladys-mystic-museum/; https://www.yelp.com/biz/bearded-ladys-mystic-museum-burbank.

The Skinny House
https://www.latimes.com/archives/la-xpm-2001-oct-29-me-63028-story.html; https://www.roadsideamerica.com/tip/9253; https://www.cbsnews.com/media/9-of-the-narrowest-homes-in-the-world/.

***The Beach Boys* Monument**
http://ohp.parks.ca.gov/?page_id=21427; https://www.deseretnews.com/article/600138537/Historical-landmark-honors-Beach-Boys.html; https://www.thebeachboys.com/content/about; https://www.washingtonpost.com/news/answer-sheet/wp/2018/01/16/the-beach-boys-brian-wilson-got-an-f-on-a-high-school-music-paper-at-75-he-just-got-it-changed-to-an-a/?utm_term=.2cc78d6970b6; http://blogs.dailybreeze.com/history/2014/03/29/fosters-old-fashioned-freeze/.

Vermonica
https://www.sheilaklein.com/projects/vermonica/vermonica.html; https://www.latimes.com/archives/la-xpm-1993-06-04-ca-43068-story.html; https://www.latimes.com/entertainment/arts/miranda/la-et-cam-vermonica-sculpture-moved-20171130-htmlstory.html; https://www.timeout.com/los-angeles/blog/before-urban-light-there-was-vermonica-110316; https://la.curbed.com/2018/8/1/17635608/streetlamps-urban-light-history-design; http://bsl.lacity.org/museum.html.

Avenue of the Athletes
https://www.latimes.com/archives/la-xpm-1985-10-10-gl-15921-story.html; https://www.zocalopublicsquare.org/2016/08/04/l-a-s-forgotten-avenue-of-the-athletes/chronicles/where-i-go/.

The Butterflies of Abandoned Surfridge
https://www.latimes.com/local/la-xpm-2013-mar-02-la-me-surfridge-20130303-story.html; https://www.kcrw.com/culture/shows/curious-coast/the-ghost-town-by-the-beach; https://southbay.goldenstate.is/paradise-lost-the-rise-fall-of-surfridge/; https://www.biologicaldiversity.org/

campaigns/esa_works/profile_pages/ElSegundoBlueButterfly.html; https://www.youtube.com/
watch?v=U4UIujUMuRk; https://www.latimes.com/local/california/la-me-ln-lax-ghost-town-preserve-
20190218-story.html.

Lost Spirits Distillery
https://www.lostspirits.net/; https://www.smithsonianmag.com/travel/mad-scientists-booze-recreating-
spirits-going-back-era-paul-revere-180971630/; https://www.timeout.com/los-angeles/blog/this-
distillery-tour-is-like-a-boozy-theme-park-for-adults-081517.

Faces of Elysian Valley
https://www.atlasobscura.com/places/riverside-roundabout; https://greenmeme.com/RIVERSIDE-
ROUNDABOUT; https://www.wescover.com/p/sculptures-by-brian-howe-and-freyja-bardell-at-riverside-
drive-bridge-over-los-angeles-river-and-ave-20-los-angeles-ca--PrJjmoS14tM; https://archpaper.
com/2018/08/riverside-roundabout-los-angeles/#gallery-0-slide-3.

The Musical Road
https://www.destinationlancasterca.org/things-to-do/only-in-the-av/musical-road/; https://jalopnik.
com/heres-how-hondas-musical-road-in-california-was-done-wr-1819600262; https://www.wsj.com/
articles/SB122469915344259035.

Speakeasy Storage
https://www.publicstorage.com/blog/public-storage/public-storage-facilities-our-historic-landmarks/;
https://ladailymirror.com/2013/04/29/mary-mallory-hollywood-heights-organist-c-sharp-minor-
major-talent/; http://laheyday.blogspot.com/2009/01/what-went-before-3634-3636-beverly-blvd.
html; https://www.theeastsiderla.com/lifestyle/history/neighborhood-fixture-east-hollywood-s-
american-storage-building/article_9b2702fe-9502-5a7d-8cb3-6d70572ec651.html; http://creepyla.
com/2016/10/05/is-this-east-hollywood-self-storage-building-the-real-tower-of-terror/.

Camera Obscura
https://www.latimes.com/archives/la-xpm-2004-sep-09-me-surroundings9-story.html; https://www.
kcet.org/history-society/a-most-novel-attraction-the-camera-obscura-of-santa-monica; https://www.
smgov.net/Departments/CCS/content.aspx?id=39798; https://www.atlasobscura.com/places/camera-
obscura-santa-monica; https://www.camaraoscuraworld.com/en/history/.

The Bejeweled Warner Bros. Theatre
https://www.laconservancy.org/locations/downtown-jewelry-exchangewarner-bros-theatre; https://
losangelestheatres.blogspot.com/2017/09/warner-downtown.html; https://www.laconservancy.org/
locations/los-angeles-jewelry-center.

Old Town Music Hall
http://www.oldtownmusichall.org/; https://www.laconservancy.org/locations/old-town-music-hall;
https://losangeleno.com/people/edward-torres/; http://tbrnews.com/entertainment/mighty-wurlitzer-
still-going-strong-at-el-segundo-s-old/article_da4a20ce-7357-11e8-8ce0-e71e55d7a9c7.html; https://
variety.com/2020/film/news/bill-field-dead-dies-organist-old-town-music-hall-silent-films-1234698482/.

The Funkiest Chicken Shack
https://www.latimes.com/archives/la-xpm-1992-01-09-we-2232-story.html; https://www.latimes.com/
archives/la-xpm-1990-07-05-vw-323-story.html.

The Black Cat Tavern
https://www.kcet.org/shows/lost-la/the-black-cat-harbinger-of-lgbtq-civil-rights; https://www.latimes.
com/local/lanow/la-me-ln-silver-lake-black-cat-lgbtq-20170208-story.html; https://www.wehoville.
com/2014/06/05/l-s-black-cat-fight-gay-rights-got-start/.

Walt Disney's Carolwood Barn
http://carolwood.com/walts-barn/; https://www.atlasobscura.com/places/walt-disney-s-carolwood-
barn; https://disneyimaginations.com/about-imaginations/about-imagineering/; https://www.ocregister.
com/2011/03/21/exploring-walt-disneys-train-barn/.

El Alisal (The Lummis Home and Gardens)
https://www.laparks.org/historic/lummis-home-and-gardens; https://www.kcet.org/history-society/lummis-house-where-highland-parks-herald-of-the-southwest-reigned-over-his-kingdom; http://photofriends.org/a-historic-house-through-the-years-el-alisal/; http://www.museumsofthearroyo.com.

El Bordello Alexandra
https://www.latimes.com/home/hometours/la-hm-bordello-20141025-story.html; https://www.atlasobscura.com/places/el-bordello-alexandra; https://www.laweekly.com/el-bordello-alexandra-how-a-venice-beach-landmark-came-to-be/.

The Shakespeare Bridge
https://loc.gov/pictures/item/ca2911/; https://www.theeastsiderla.com/archives/neighborhood-fixture-the-shakespeare-bridge-of-los-feliz/article_ec903798-d445-5dc4-87a4-8869a371ea1a.html; https://www.kcet.org/shows/lost-la/a-brief-history-of-bridges-in-los-angeles-county; https://www.latimes.com/archives/la-xpm-1998-apr-20-me-41253-story.html.

The Dunbar Hotel and Central Avenue's Jazz Legacy
https://www.laconservancy.org/locations/dunbar-hotel; https://www.cityprojectca.org/blog/archives/689; https://savingplaces.org/stories/a-los-angeles-landmark-gets-a-second-act-dunbar-hotel-south-central-avenue#.XVRXNpNKjMU; https://www.kcet.org/history-society/when-central-avenue-swung-the-dunbar-hotel-and-the-golden-age-of-las-little-harlem; http://scalar.usc.edu/works/historic-central-avenue-los-angeles/a-brief-history-of-central-avenue; https://www.ethnomusicologyreview.ucla.edu/content/sounds-central-avenue.

Valley Relics Museum
https://valleyrelicsmuseum.org; https://www.discoverlosangeles.com/things-to-do/step-back-in-time-at-the-valley-relics-museum.

The Velaslavasay Panorama
https://panoramaonview.org/home

Biddy Mason Memorial Park
https://www.nps.gov/people/biddymason.htm; http://www.famechurch.org; https://www.laconservancy.org/sites/default/files/files/documents/Power%20of%20Place%20ch.6.pdf; https://www.laconservancy.org/locations/biddy-mason-memorial-park.

The Brown Derby
https://www.latimes.com/archives/la-xpm-2005-nov-27-me-then27-story.html; https://www.latimes.com/archives/la-xpm-1985-05-19-re-9531-story.html; https://www.latimes.com/archives/la-xpm-1985-05-19-re-9531-story.html; https://hollywoodphotographs.com/category/111-1/brown-derby-restaurant/.

Holyland Exhibition
https://www.latimes.com/archives/la-xpm-2001-sep-30-me-51701-story.html; https://www.kcet.org/shows/artbound/holyland-exhibition-a-reflection-of-a-middle-eastern-dream; https://www.latimes.com/archives/la-xpm-1997-04-11-me-47588-story.html.

St. Vincent Court
https://www.kcet.org/food/st-vincent-courts-strange-past-and-unsure-future; https://dbase1.lapl.org/webpics/calindex/documents/03/159012.pdf; http://www.thedepartmentstoremuseum.org/2010/05/bullocks.html; http://pcad.lib.washington.edu/building/9453/; http://www.ladowntownnews.com/news/the-school-the-city-forgot/article_d7d0b4ce-ef9f-57b3-8bb5-702a33b35ec7.html; https://www.californiahistoricallandmarks.com/landmarks/chl-567.

Outer Limits Tattoo
https://www.outerlimitstattoo.com/full-history-of-long-beach-tattoo-shop; https://ocweekly.com/from-bert-grimm-to-outer-limits-this-long-beach-tattoo-shop-remains-the-oldest-in-the-world-7012957/; https://www.kcet.org/shows/lost-la/a-walk-along-long-beachs-gaudy-tawdry-bawdy-pike.

The Santa Monica Mosaic House

https://www.custommosaicart.com/; https://www.latimes.com/local/la-me-c1-tile-house-20140127-dto-htmlstory.html.

The Theme Building at LAX

https://www.latimes.com/local/california/la-me-retrospective-lax-20151126-story.html; https://www.laconservancy.org/locations/theme-building-lax; https://www.latimes.com/travel/la-tr-travel-lax-theme-building-hotel-idea-future-20190612-story.html.

Ballerina Clown

http://www.borofsky.com/index.php?album=ballerinaclown; https://www.latimes.com/entertainment/arts/culture/la-et-cm-review-jonathan-borofskys-ballerina-clown-20140518-column.html; http://www.lincolnandrose.com/home/ballerina-clown-kicking-again; http://www.getty.edu/publications/keepitmoving/posters/17-erhan/.

A Brewery's Batchelder Tiles

https://angelcitybrewery.com/wtf-batchelder-tiles/; https://la.curbed.com/2017/3/3/14781266/angel-city-brewery-history; https://www.curbed.com/2014/7/9/10080352/century-old-batchelder-tiles-ignite-las-preservationists; https://www.laconservancy.org/sites/default/files/files/documents/ArtsDistrict_Booklet_LR.pdf; https://www.smithsonianmag.com/smart-news/saving-los-angeles-batchelder-tile-180952002/; https://pasadenahistory.org/collections/batchelder-part-1/; https://pasadenahistory.org/research-and-collections/batchelder-registry/; https://www.discoverlosangeles.com/event/2019/06/15/angel-city-art-tours-new-weekends-at-1pm; https://angelcitybrewery.com/wtf-is-that-the-slide/.

Ferndell Nature Museum

https://www.friendsofgriffithpark.org/saving-historic-fern-dell/; https://nhm.org/stories/scoop-ferndell-griffith-parks-enchanted-nature-museum; https://www.latimes.com/local/la-xpm-2012-feb-19-la-me-ferndell-facelift-20120219-story.html; https://www.hikespeak.com/trails/ferndell-trail-griffith-park-western-canyon/; https://time.com/3881383/marilyn-monroe-early-photos-los-angeles-1950/.

The Coca-Cola Oceanliner

https://www.latimes.com/archives/la-xpm-2002-aug-22-me-surround22-story.html; https://www.coca-colacompany.com/stories/landmark-coca-cola-building-at-heart-of-l-a--neighborhoods-rebir; https://www.latimes.com/business/la-fi-honey-lease-20180801-story.html.

Neon Retro Arcade

http://www.neonretroarcade.com/; https://www.sgvtribune.com/2018/01/16/neon-retro-arcade-expands-with-new-location-in-northridge/.

Capitol Records Morse Code

https://www.discoverlosangeles.com/visit/the-capitol-records-building-the-story-of-an-la-icon; https://www.laconservancy.org/locations/capitol-records-tower; https://www.lamag.com/citythinkblog/vintage-los-angeles-its-christmastime-at-the-capitol-records-building/; https://www.latimes.com/opinion/la-xpm-2013-jul-17-la-oe-naidorf-capitol-records-hollywood-development-20130717-story.html; https://www.archdaily.com/804265/the-record-company-headquarters-that-revived-1950s-hollywood-with-iconic-architecture.

The Great Los Angeles Air Raid

https://www.smithsonianmag.com/history/great-los-angeles-air-raid-terrified-citizenseven-though-no-bombs-were-dropped-180967890/; http://www.ftmac.org/AirRaid2019_Advsale.htm; http://www.theairraid.com/; https://www.latimes.com/visuals/framework/la-me-fw-archives-1942-battle-la-20170221-story.html.

Highland Park Bowl

https://laist.com/news/food/highland-park-bowl; https://laist.com/news/food/photos-the-new-highland-park-bowl; https://www.highlandparkbowl.com; https://www.latimes.com/archives/la-xpm-1995-08-13-ls-34589-story.html; https://la.curbed.com/2016/5/6/11606218/highland-park-bowl-restoration; https://archive.kpcc.org/programs/offramp/2016/04/25/48108/photos-mr-t-s-bowl-in-highland-park-stripped-back; https://www.instagram.com/p/BHQtlFIBfOz/?hl=en.

Llano Del Rio

https://www.latimes.com/archives/la-xpm-1989-05-28-me-1544-story.html; https://www.californiahistoricallandmarks.com/landmarks/chl-933; https://la.curbed.com/2017/5/1/15465616/utopia-socialist-los-angeles-llano-del-rio; https://www.kcet.org/shows/lost-la/llano-del-rio-from-utopia-to-ghost-town; https://www.kcet.org/shows/lost-la/red-flags-over-los-angeles-part-i-socialism-and-the-election-of-1911; http://www.getty.edu/news/press/center/hockney_pearblossom.html https://alexwesterman.com/visual-arts/david-hockneys-pearblossom-highway; https://www.ic.org/llanodelrio; https://www.kqed.org/news/10340904/100-years-later-californias-lost-commune-comes-briefly-back-to-life; https://www.thedesertway.com/llano-del-rio.

The Hollyhock House

http://www.barnsdallartpark.com/activities.asp#hollyhockhouse; https://www.laconservancy.org/locations/hollyhock-house; https://la.curbed.com/2015/2/13/9992116/frank-lloyd-wright-los-angeles-hollyhock.

California Institute of Abnormal Arts

https://www.laweekly.com/it-doesnt-get-any-weirder-than-this-north-hollywood-spot/; https://www.atlasobscura.com/places/california-institute-for-the-abnormalarts-cia; https://www.facebook.com/CIAbnormalarts/.

Route 66: End of the Trail

https://www.lamag.com/askchris/ever-wondered-route-66-ends/; https://www.roadsideamerica.com/story/27318; http://smlocalhistory.blogspot.com/2011/07/penguin-coffee-shop.html.

The Victorians of Carroll Avenue

https://www.laconservancy.org/events/angelino-heights-walking-tour; https://www.laconservancy.org/locations/haskins-house; https://www.laconservancy.org/locations/innes-house; https://www.laconservancy.org/locations/sessions-house; https://dbase1.lapl.org/webpics/calindex/documents/02/17358.pdf; http://historicechopark.org/history-landmarks/places-landmarks/angelino-heights/; https://la.curbed.com/maps/los-angeles-victorian-architecture-styles-map; https://www.latimes.com/archives/la-xpm-2002-may-30-me-surround30-story.html; https://www.lamag.com/citythinkblog/scene-thriller-house/; https://preservation.lacity.org/hpoz/la/angelino-heights.

Looff's Lite-a-Line

https://lbpost.com/news/business/looff-s-lite-a-line-a-shrine-to-long-beach-s-amusement-past; https://www.latimes.com/archives/la-xpm-2004-nov-25-me-surrounding25-story.html; https://wizardofodds.com/games/lite-a-line/; https://www.atlasobscura.com/places/looff-s-lite-a-line; https://www.latimes.com/archives/la-xpm-1985-09-22-hl-18489-story.html; http://www.historyofcarousels.com/carousel-history/charles-i-d-looff/; https://www.laweekly.com/the-1-20-thrill-ride-looffs-lite-a-line/; https://wizardofodds.com/games/lite-a-line/.

The Los Angeles Breakfast Club

http://www.labreakfastclub.com/; https://www.kcet.org/food-living/the-strangest-club-in-los-angeles-the-la-breakfast-club.

Whisky & Poetry Salon

http://www.whiskyandpoetrysalon.com/; https://www.ardentspirits.la/.

Toyo Miyatake's Camera

http://www.publicartinla.com/Downtown/Little_Tokyo/miyatake.html; https://blog.janm.org/2015/03/24/toyo-miyatakes-camera-captured-japanese-american-history/; https://www.kcet.org/shows/departures/toyo-miyatake-preserving-history-through-a-lens; https://www.kcet.org/shows/lost-la/toyo-miyatake-capturing-the-stories-of-japanese-americans-in-la; http://www.publicartinla.com/Downtown/Little_Tokyo/omoide1.html; http://www.publicartinla.com/Downtown/Little_Tokyo/miyatake1.html; https://laist.com/2014/12/09/when_santa_anita_racetrack_was_a_ja.php; https://www.yelp.com/biz/toyo-miyatakes-camera-los-angeles; https://www.latimes.com/archives/la-xpm-1993-08-01-ci-19502-story.html; https://www.nps.gov/museum/exhibits/manz/exb/Camp/DailyLife/MANZ3331_camera.html.

Astronaut Islands

https://la.curbed.com/2018/9/28/17858248/history-long-beach-oil-islands-thums; https://longbeachmarinas. net/long-beach-oil-islands/; https://aoghs.org/technology/thums-california-hidden-oil-islands/; https://www. theatlantic.com/photo/2014/08/the-urban-oil-fields-of-los-angeles/100799/; https://www.stand.la/history-of-oil-in-los-angeles.html; https://www.lamag.com/citythinkblog/hidden-oil-wells/.

Crossroads of the World

https://www.crossroadsoftheworldla.com/; https://www.laconservancy.org/locations/crossroads-world; https://www.kcet.org/history-society/bloody-commerce-crossroads-of-the-world-and-the-murder-of-the-decade; https://la.curbed.com/2019/1/22/18193330/hollywood-crossroads-world-redevelopment-city-council-approved; https://www.latimes.com/books/la-ca-jc-taschen-la-office-crossroads-20190222-story.html.

The Grapes of Avila Adobe

http://www.ucanr.org/blogs/blogcore/postdetail.cfm?postnum=3148; https://ucanr.edu/blogs/ blogcore/postdetail.cfm?postnum=4284; https://elpueblo.lacity.org/history; https://www.scpr.org/ news/2016/05/20/60818/making-wine-from-a-piece-of-l-a-s-early-history/; https://www.latimes.com/ food/drinks/la-fo-0919-pueblo-20150919-story.html.

The Max Factor Building

https://www.beautylish.com/a/vxspr/the-history-of-max-factor; http://thehollywoodmuseum.com/ about/our-history-vision/; https://www.huffpost.com/entry/where-lucy-became-a-redhe_b_5135896; http://onlyinhollywood.org/hollywood-museum-history-inside/; https://www.latimes.com/archives/la-xpm-1996-06-09-mn-13311-story.html; https://makeup.lovetoknow.com/max-factor-pancake-makeup; https://blog.fidmmuseum.org/museum/2017/02/max-factor.html.

Happy Foot/Sad Foot Sign

https://ericbrightwell.com/2019/09/09/art-in-the-streets-the-happy-foot-sad-foot-sign-1986-2019/; https://www.theeastsiderla.com/neighborhoods/silver_lake/a-sign-of-silver-lake-is-gone-the-happy-foot/article_5d6ebef6-d02c-11e9-a56c-bfd3eceab0d4.html; https://www.lamag.com/culturefiles/ yachts-lastest-music-video-ode-happy-foot-sad-foot-sign/; https://losangeleno.com/strange-days/happy-foot-sad-foot/; https://www.latimes.com/business/la-fi-happy-foot-sad-foot-moving-20190712-story. html; https://www.latimes.com/archives/la-xpm-2010-jul-01-la-me-0701-tobar-20100701-story.html; https://www.theeastsiderla.com/neighborhoods/los_feliz/happy-foot-sad-foot-sign-moves-to-a-new-home/article_10b76924-e26e-11e9-bc2d-9be15623a78f.html.

The Boyle Hotel

https://www.laconservancy.org/locations/boyle-hotel; https://www.nps.gov/articles/boyle-hotel-ca. htm; http://boyleheightshistoryblog.blogspot.com/2014/09/historic-photos-of-boyle-heights.html; https://librosschmibros.wordpress.com/; https://la.streetsblog.org/2012/03/09/a-long-history-of-creating-a-sense-of-place-at-las-latino-triangle-parks-mariachi-plaza/; https://mariachiplazalosangeles. com/site/; https://www.kcet.org/history-society/the-shifting-cultures-of-multiracial-boyle-heights; https://barrioboychik.com/2018/11/22/the-first-displacement-the-indigenous-people-of-boyle-heights/; https://www.latimes.com/local/la-xpm-2012-sep-04-la-me-mariachi-hotel-20120904-story.html.

LA's Hidden Religious Wall

https://www.laeruv.com/; https://www.lamag.com/citythinkblog/100-square-miles-los-angeles-surrounded-hidden-religious-wall/; http://valleyeruv.org/; https://www.kcrw.com/culture/shows/design-and-architecture/west-las-eruv-the-hidden-wall-built-and-maintained-by-orthodox-jews; https://www. laeruv.com/in-the-news/la-times-kindred-spirits-can-call-this-place-home/; https://www.tripsavvy.com/ discovering-jewish-los-angeles-1587019; https://www.hmdb.org/m.asp?m=122688.

The Witch's House

https://www.lamag.com/citythinkblog/exclusive-look-inside-witchs-house-beverly-hills/; https://laist. com/2016/10/27/photos_beverly_hills_witch_house_spadena.php; https://www.latimes.com/local/la-hm-storybook13jan13-story.html; culvercityhistoricalsociety.org/articles/willat-studios-in-early-culver-city/.

The Batcave

https://modernhiker.com/hike/bronson-caves/; https://www.hikespeak.com/trails/bronson-cave/; https://www.latimes.com/archives/la-xpm-1996-04-16-ls-58904-story.html; http://www.weirdca.com/location.php?location=686.

The Bunny Museum

http://www.thebunnymuseum.com/; https://www.latimes.com/home/la-hm-bunny-museum-20180322-htmlstory.html; https://www.guinnessworldrecords.com/world-records/largest-collection-of-rabbits-(bunnies).

The Lizard People beneath Fort Moore

https://www.lamag.com/citythinkblog/citydig-the-underground-catacombs-of-las-lizard-people/; https://losangeleno.com/strange-days/lizard-people/; https://www.latimes.com/la-sh-lizard-people-throwback-thursday-20140123-story.html; https://bigthink.com/strange-maps/443-secret-caves-of-the-lizard-people; https://www.kcet.org/history-society/the-many-lives-of-fort-moore-hill-the-shifting-and-shrinking-of-a-los-angeles-icon; http://www.laalmanac.com/mysterious/my02.php; https://latimesblogs.latimes.com/.a/6a00d8341c630a53ef01157020df2e970b-pi; https://latimespast.tumblr.com/post/74283915119/lizard-people; https://latimesblogs.latimes.com/thedailymirror/2009/04/gold-hunters-dig-for-lost-underground-empire-of-the-lizard-people.html.

Hollywood Heritage Museum

https://www.hollywoodheritage.org/; https://www.latimes.com/entertainment/classichollywood/la-ca-mn-classic-hollywood-20150823-story.html; https://www.kcet.org/shows/lost-la/before-the-movies-came-hollywood-was-a-rustic-country-town; http://www.hollywoodheritage.com/news/HHI_Newsletter_2013_v32-n3.pdf.

Beverly Hot Springs

https://www.latimes.com/archives/la-xpm-1987-08-31-me-3255-story.html; http://beverlyhotsprings.com/history/.

Los Angeles Pet Memorial Park

https://lapetcemetery.com/; https://www.latimes.com/local/la-me-c1-pet-cemetery-20131025-dto-htmlstory.html; https://www.kcet.org/history-society/happier-hunting-grounds-the-los-angeles-pet-memorial-park-in-calabasas.

Tankland

http://tankland.com/.

Laserium

http://laserium.com/who-is-laserium/; http://www.laserium.org/music/chronological.html; https://www.lamag.com/culturefiles/l-s-forgotten-laser-emporium-will-take-back-70s/; https://www.timeout.com/los-angeles/blog/laserium-las-original-laser-light-show-is-back; https://wearethemutants.com/2016/08/18/laserium-brochure-circa-1977/; http://spacewatchtower.blogspot.com/2013/11/laserium-40th-anniversary.html; http://www.laserfest.org/news/opn-laser-shows.pdf.

The Lost Zoos and Animal Farms of LA

https://www.kcet.org/history-society/a-whimpering-roar-the-old-griffith-park-zoo-then-and-now; https://www.lamag.com/citythinkblog/colorful-history-los-angeles-zoo/; http://www.laalmanac.com/environment/ev702.php#sketch; https://homesteadmuseum.wordpress.com/2017/10/04/lions-and-ostriches-and-gators-oh-my-los-angeles-animal-farms-in-the-1920s/; https://www.friendsofgriffithpark.org/griffith-park-zoo-the-great-world-zoo-that-never-was-1912-1966/; https://www.latimes.com/archives/la-xpm-2009-may-14-me-selig-zoo-lions14-story.html; https://www.lamag.com/citythinkblog/citydig-the-ostriches-of-griffith-park/; https://www.atlasobscura.com/places/cawston-ostrich-farm; https://www.lapl.org/collections-resources/blogs/lapl/birds-feather; https://www.lapl.org/collections-resources/blogs/lapl/bring-kids-fun-california-alligator-farm; https://laist.com/2009/01/24/laistory_monkey_island.php; https://www.latimes.com/archives/la-xpm-2009-may-14-me-selig-zoo-lions14-story.html.

The Original Speakeasies

http://www.ladowntownnews.com/news/downtowns-prohibition-history/article_73350d22-3c82-11ea-9ecc-37888bcc24a6.html; https://www.kcet.org/shows/lost-la/how-alcohol-still-seeped-into-los-angeles-during-prohibition; https://www.kcet.org/food/the-illegal-years-of-the-del-monte-speakeasy; http://www.cartwheelart.com/tours/underground-la-tour/.

Camouflaged Airports

https://www.lockheedmartin.com/en-us/news/features/history/camouflage.html; https://www.latimes.com/archives/la-xpm-2002-aug-04-me-then4-story.html; https://warfarehistorynetwork.com/daily/wwii/wonderland-the-fake-cities-on-americas-west-coast/; https://www.latimes.com/local/lanow/la-me-santa-monica-airport-20170128-story.html; https://www.smgov.net/departments/airport/history.aspx; https://www.museumofflying.org/; https://www.airspacemag.com/flight-today/can-airport-be-saved-180952758/; https://santamonicahistory.org/exhibits/from-biplanes-to-bombers/; https://www.latimes.com/local/lanow/la-me-santa-monica-airport-20170128-story.html.

The Sprawling Wistaria Vine

https://www.latimes.com/home/la-hm-wistaria-festival-20180317-story.html; https://www.sierramadrechamber.com/blank; https://www.pasadenastarnews.com/2014/03/10/sierra-madres-120-year-old-world-record-holding-vine-on-display-during-wistaria-festival/; https://www.scpr.org/news/2014/03/14/42794/how-did-sierra-madre-s-record-setting-wisteria-get/; https://breathelighter.wordpress.com/tag/seven-horticultural-wonders-of-the-world/; https://www.kcet.org/shows/huell-howser/classic-huell-the-vine.

The Pink Motel

https://la.curbed.com/2017/8/11/16135148/pink-motel-netflix-glow; https://cadillac-jacks.com/About-Us.htm; https://www.laconservancy.org/locations/cadillac-jacks-and-pink-motel; http://www.iamnotastalker.com/2015/03/24/the-pink-motel-from-vanderpump-rules/; https://www.facebook.com/ThePinkMotel/.

Hotel Figueroa

https://www.hotelfigueroa.com/our-hotel/history/; https://www.latimes.com/designla/la-design-la-hotel-figueroa-20181126-story.html; https://www.cnn.com/travel/article/hotel-figueroa-women-los-angeles/index.html; https://www.kcet.org/history-society/the-figueroa-hotel-the-surprising-feminist-origins-of-a-sexy-downtown-staple.

The Lotus Festival

http://historicechopark.org/history-landmarks/places-landmarks/echo-park-lake-lotus-bed/; https://www.lotusfestivalla.org/test; https://latimes.newspapers.com/image/380645944/?terms=%22echo%2Bpark%2Blake%22%2B%22lotus%22; https://www.latimes.com/local/lanow/la-me-ln-lotus-festival-returns-to-echo-park-lake-20140712-story.html; https://www.latimes.com/local/la-me-lotus-echo-park-20130606-dto-htmlstory.html; http://www.echoparknow.com/2010/07/10/brief-history-of-the-lotus-festival/; https://www.kcet.org/shows/lost-la/echo-parks-lake-began-as-a-drinking-water-reservoir.

Rancho Los Alamitos

https://www.rancholosalamitos.com/history.html; https://www.c-span.org/video/?407566-1/rancho-los-alamitos; https://www.laconservancy.org/locations/rancho-los-alamitos; https://www.kcet.org/travel/chasing-down-las-rancho-era-past.

Norton Sales, Inc.

http://nortonsalesinc.com/index.html; https://www.latimes.com/archives/la-xpm-2007-mar-25-sci-junkyard25-story.html; https://docs.google.com/document/d/1SLL5rCs5rFjBIxSguEDeU2rZ6pTeozi6vtmRD3fmmv0/edit; https://docs.google.com/document/d/1TeoLHIQCK2bDYv7veT7O0shiEem2orC-D1AeRP1fASs/edit.

The William Mulholland Memorial Fountain

https://www.kcet.org/history-society/the-mulholland-memorial-fountain-a-grand-monument-to-a-man-and-water; https://waterandpower.org/museum/Mulholland_Monuments.html; http://publicartinla.com/sculptures/mulholland_park.html; https://www.archpaper.com/2013/11/los-angeles-celebrates-aqueduct-centennial-with-interactive-garden/; https://thereitistakeit.org/.

Greystone Mansion

https://www.greystonemansion.org/history.html; https://www.kcet.org/history-society/we-shall-never-know-murder-money-and-the-enduring-mystery-of-greystone-mansion; https://www.latimes.com/local/lanow/la-me-ln-doheny-murder-20190216-story.html; https://www.lapl.org/collections-resources/blogs/lapl/if-these-walls-could-talk

Secret Gardens

https://www.musiccenter.org/visit/Our-Venues/Our-Outdoor-Venues/; https://www.atlasobscura.com/places/garden-of-oz; https://www.jaccc.org/james-irvine-japanese-garden; https://www.botgard.ucla.edu/; https://www.peacelabyrinth.org/.

The Bison of Catalina

https://www.catalinaconservancy.org/index.php?s=news&p=article_24; https://www.catalinaconservancy.org/index.php?s=news&p=article_25; https://www.visitcatalinaisland.com/blog/post/buffalo-milk-the-official-drink-of-catalina-island/; https://www.lovecatalina.com/blog/post/william-wrigley-jr/.

The Wayfarers Chapel

https://www.wayfarerschapel.org/about/history/; https://www.laconservancy.org/locations/wayfarers-chapel ;https://npgallery.nps.gov/GetAsset/5a7d29ce-7663-4cc4-af60-996853862e14/; https://www.atlasobscura.com/places/wayfarers-chapel.

Hidden Staircases

http://historicechopark.org/history-landmarks/places-landmarks/echo-park-stairways/; https://www.secretstairs-la.com/welcome.html; https://www.latimes.com/la-la-walks-music-box-steps-20141017-htmlstory.html; https://www.latimes.com/archives/la-xpm-2003-aug-21-me-surround21-story.html; http://streetcar.la/project-info/streetcar-history/; https://socalstairclimbers.com/.

The Bruce Lee Statue

https://www.latimes.com/local/lanow/la-xpm-2013-jun-16-la-me-ln-bruce-lee-statue-unveiled-in-las-chinatown-20130616-story.html; https://www.latimes.com/archives/la-xpm-1998-aug-17-ca-13848-story.html; https://www.nbclosangeles.com/news/bruce-lee-studio-reopens-in-chinatown/1966970/; https://www.lamag.com/culturefiles/bruce-lee-chinatown/; https://www.ericcarrjkd.com/; https://www.laweekly.com/bruce-lees-huge-bronze-statue-turns-into-a-mecca-in-l-a-s-chinatown-video/; https://brucelee.com/bruce-lee; https://www.facebook.com/BruceLee/posts/10160906626185634.

The Ruins of Mt. Lowe Railway

http://www.mountlowe.org/mount-lowe-history/history-of-the-mount-lowe-incline-railway/; http://www.thaddeuslowe.name/MLEchohouse.htm; https://gamblehouse.org/altadenas-famous-mount-lowe-railway/; https://californiathroughmylens.com/echo-mountain-hike; https://waterandpower.org/museum/Mt_Lowe_Railway.html.

The Oviatt Building

https://www.laconservancy.org/locations/oviatt-building; https://www.kcet.org/history-society/the-james-oviatt-building-the-bespoke-brilliance-and-pretension-behind-an-art-deco; https://www.latimes.com/local/la-xpm-2012-aug-09-la-me-harnisch-chevalier-20120809-story.html; https://www.latimes.com/archives/la-xpm-2004-jan-13-fi-oviatt13-story.html; https://www.latimes.com/archives/la-xpm-2000-sep-10-me-18730-story.html; https://www.latimes.com/archives/la-xpm-1988-06-05-re-6326-story.html; https://www.lamag.com/citythinkblog/scene-it-before-hotel-cortez-from-american-horror-story-hotel/; http://www.cicadaclub.com/.

The Missing Canals of Venice

https://www.westland.net/venicehistory/articles/kinney.htm; https://argonautnews.com/the-secret-life-of-abbot-kinney/; https://www.kcet.org/shows/lost-la/the-lost-canals-of-venice-of-america; https://www.abbotkinneyblvd.com/about-abbot-kinney; https://www.westland.net/venice/history.htm.

INDEX

198

199